PRAISE FOR THE WORK OF PHILIP BRADY

Forged Correspondences

Wildly inventive, these 'forgeries' roam from Heraclitus to the Queen of Sheba, from Newark to Africa. Highly serious and richly comic, a great trip.   —Maxine Kumin, *Ploughshares*

This book is a journey through glittering empires of the imagination.   —David Citino

Philip Brady's *Forged Correspondences* has been written in blood by a poet who is a brother to the dispossessed ... This powerful book is a tour of personal and historical plague country; no reader will escape from it unscathed, unchanged, or, by way of that complex effect and gift of the most serious and accomplished art, ungrateful.   —William Heyen

Weal

The poems in Philip Brady's *Weal* engage us with dazzling language and intellectual range and a lovely music ... Brady's voice is zany, rough and heartbreaking and *Weal* is full of wild surprises.   —Maggie Anderson

Philip Brady's *Weal* gives a powerful account of one man's journey through this world.... One looks up from these pages a little wiser, a little more alert, a little readier to carry on.
                              —Richard Tillinghast

This is an unpredictable, demanding, strong, book, each poem an exploration.   —Milton Kessler

ALSO BY PHILIP BRADY

Poetry

Plague Country (chapbook), 1990

Forged Correspondences, 1996

Weal, 2000

Criticism

Critical Essays on
James Joyce's Portrait of the Artist as a Young Man,
(co-edited with James F. Carens)

TO PROVE MY BLOOD

A Tale of Emigrations & the Afterlife

by Philip Brady

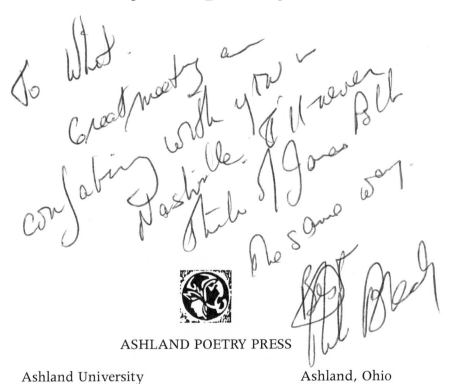

ASHLAND POETRY PRESS

Ashland University   Ashland, Ohio

Brady, Philip, 1955-
   To prove my blood : a tale of emigrations & the
afterlife / by Philip Brady. -- Ashland, Ohio : Ashland
Poetry Press, 2003.
   p. cm.
   LCCN 2003103870
   ISBN 0-912592-50-8

   1. Brady, Philip, 1955---Family. 2. Irish Americans
--Biography. 3. New York (N.Y.)--Biography. 4. Peace
Corps (U.S.)--Africa. 5. Police--New York (State) New
York. 6. Crimmins, Alice--Trials, litigation, etc.
7. Ohio--Biography.   I. Title.

PS3552.R2437P76 2003   813'.6
                      QBI33-1435

Cover Painting "Not Knowing, Relying on Intuition," by Robert Carioscia

Design by Elizabeth Woll

IN MEMORIAM

Philip & Anne Brady

1918-1994

I have no child, I have nothing but a book—

Nothing but that to prove your blood and mine.

—W. B. YEATS

CONTENTS

CONTENTS

ACKNOWLEDGMENTS

"First Born" was first published in *West Branch*. It also appeared in *Forged Correspondences*, New Myths, 1996.

"Wiretap" was first published in *New Myths/Mss*, and later appeared in *Forged Correspondences*.

"Lagos" was first published in *The Alembic*, and was reprinted in *Weal*, Ashland Poetry Press, 2000.

Thanks are due to Youngstown State University for a Research Professorship, which permitted me time to write.

As always, deepest gratitude to the greater maker, Robert Mooney, for his guidance and encouragement at every step, and to Linda Strom, who believed.

The McCann sisters, Brooklyn, 1922

TO PROVE MY BLOOD

A Tale of Emigrations & the Afterlife

PROLOGUE

ARACHNE

Arachne starts with Ovid and finishes with me.
—MICHAEL LONGLEY

WHO would have thought, in 1960, when my brother's birth cramped our row house, expelling Aunt Mary back to Brooklyn, that a fat slice of the century later hers would be the last penny the McCanns would spend? Brooklyn should have made a quick end to her, but she flourished. At the age of sixty-one, Mary Martin began a career as a cleaning lady at the Borough Hall Board of Education, clanking through plaster labyrinths, shouldering fire doors, palming ashtrays, and single-handedly reviving the myth of an era when every brownstone boasted its Irish maid.

"Hey, Mary," the suits would tease, as she flicked her dust mop through olive cubicles, "You're doing a great job there. Rubbing like you're going to conjure a genie."

"Show me the bottle, Gorgeous," she'd rattle back. "It would take that baldy fella to clean your dirt."

She had them on a string—the psychologists and specialists, the social workers and the Ph.D.s. Everyone turned to her for proof that a primeval Brooklyn still shadowed.

And in September 1966, when brother Brian toddled off to St. Kevin's first-grade, even my mother turned to Mary. Alone all day, my mother felt our six rooms shrink to the size of bouillon cubes. The rut she dug to drain off entropy—a wash, a sweat with Jack LaLane, a smoke with tea—soon sludged with livid waste. She tippled, she waked her girlhood, and finally, her nerves stretched until she had to scream or flee.

I was eleven, used to the phone calls my mother made to Brooklyn nightly since Mary'd been packed off, how she'd climb the stairs, sit cross-legged on the bed and light a cigarette, cradling the receiver in the crook of her neck. Sometimes I'd trail after her, badgering about school or toys, while Mary's voice, amped by Ma Bell, poured into her other ear.

"I had the toast, y'know," Mary'd sing. "The rye toast, at the Meyer's Deli. The bread's gorgeous. There's a new man at the counter. A new Jewish man, with the quiff and the funny hat, y'know. At the counter. A terrible hum coming off his greatcoat, Pet, like mousy cheese!"

"That's nice, Mary, and did you shop today?"

"Not a bit of it. Well, I was at the Woolworth's, y'know, on Grand Street, with the dollar sign. 'Tis dear, Pet, the Woolworth's is, disgraceful, shag the coupons, and Pet, you can't tell boys from girls with the nests of hair. . . ."

But one night, my mother broke through, wrangled the old woman from her litany of chores and toast, and stirred a memory of childhood when Mary had fed and washed her baby sister, her Pet, twenty years her junior. How, I don't know. But whatever prayer she uttered, it was heard, and it set Mary spinning her one plot: to save her sister by bringing her back to Brooklyn.

"A rare thing, a quare talent altogether," Mary hummed, fiddling her brush over the braided yarmulke of Dr. Rosenshein. "It's in the fingers, you see, Doctor. She's always had it."

Her wenned hands fluttered in another world, inches from his beard. "Why, she taps letters the way Paderewski plays piano. And a smile like my Pet's! She'd be the best secretary in the world."

And so Anne Brady, née McCann, youngest of four girls ferried from Ulster in 1922, dubbed "Pet" in the ur-time of Brooklyn, followed her eldest sister on their youthward journey over the

Kosciusko Bridge. She made a great success (her smile demonstrating the required teeth) and was appointed clerk at Borough Hall, where her touted fingers dipped into the pork barrel her sister had pried open.

But it didn't stop there. One evening at the dinner table a month after my mother started her new job, my father announced that he'd been fingered for something big. He was leaving the Police Force to be top bird for a new Fingerprint Security System at 110 Livingstone Street in the Brooklyn Borough Hall Board of Education. He winked at his stunned fiefdom, swiping his martini over the meatloaf. The matter was being considered. It was being handled personally by a nabob at the Board of Ed., a gentleman by the name of Dr. Joel S. Rosenshein.

Did my father trace his apotheosis to Aunt Mary? Did he suspect that returning her to Brooklyn from her seat in the parlor wingback of 53-28 194th Street, Flushing, precipitated a kind of continental drifting, leading inexorably toward me, toward what I'm left with now, in Ohio, childless, the rain lashing outside and a great bare oak rising from the earth in a frozen rage of limbs?

It was his job to trace, but anyone sheathed in flesh for very long begins to sense that some clues need to be processed by a special organ, an internal reality filter stuck in there somewhere between chakras, and in my father this organ was as tough as a boxing glove and strong enough to metabolize whole fifths of lethal facts.

But for all his fantasies, his swagger, his limericks, and his garlanded swivel chair in the Borough Hall Board of Education, it's not him, and not his wife, and none of the litter of Eumenides begotten to Ulster and spirited west by Francis and Sarah McCann, but only the eldest, Mary Martin, who's survived.

She's still here, living in a nursing home down the street from me, eking the last few moments from the century whose first light spawned her. And though she's dwindled to a nerveless thing, shriven of memory, in the afternoons she taps her foot softly on her wheelchair's pad, as if warming to an antediluvian reel.

And though the four McCann girls propagated diligently with their share of the navvies, lollards, cops, and narrowbacks of Irish Brooklyn, mine is the only shadow clinging to the last quicksilver of a breathing dream. I'm the only one enwebbed in myth, craving to spin and also to break free, to make and to make up. And what is it I would spin or break? What's flesh anyway, especially to me, whose office is to watch its arachnid shriveling? Maybe it's death I have to spin out of myself—out of my fear, my craving. Maybe these words offer the only hope for Mary Martin née McCann to start the long swim back through time.

PART ONE

NAMED FOR SORROW

To bury the dead we must first unearth them.
—Thomas Lynch

1.

MYTH & UNCERTAINTY

But what else
Can a mother give her daughter but such
Beautiful rifts in time?

—Eavan Boland

ALTHOUGH Aunt Mary moved back to Brooklyn after Brian's birth, she was never really gone; she merely faded to a voice humming in the phone, though it seldom occurred to me to listen. Now that she's the last sister alive, spirited to Ohio to live down the block, now that I want to hear all that she could teach, she's not really here.

It's a paradox that my students, studying Heisenberg in "Myth & Science," might appreciate. According to his Uncertainty Principle, no one knows where anything is at a given time, but every Monday-Wednesday-Friday at 8 a.m. on my way to class I drive the same three blocks and take the same elevator and tramp to the same room where the same ninety-five-year-old woman, my link to myth, snores. I bring cafeteria tea to her bedside and recall her to her fate. If she knows me, she takes the cup, and thanks me, calls me "son." But some mornings, she wakes to Heisenberg—white beard, skull gaunt as a key.

3

"Where's Flip?" she cries; "Where's my nephew?"

"It's alright, Aunt Mary, it's me."

"Oh, Gorgeous. What a face on you," she sniffs, then bursts into laughter.

Mary Martin knows all about uncertainty. In 1924, when Dick Martin, Belfast Presbyterian, died of stomach cancer at the age of twenty-nine, his Papist widow Mary made no trouble about returning obediently to childhood. There was no question of remaining in the gardener's cottage of the Long Island estate where her husband had worked; she simply left with her baby daughter for her parents' Brooklyn railroad flat. Even when Dick Martin's parents crossed the water like God's wrath, it was not Mary but my grandmother who barred the door and kept the Martins from taking Mary's infant back to Ulster. And if Mary couldn't hold on to the shirttail of a Protestant too feckless to stay alive, she wasn't about to seek another man.

"You never know what you might get," she told me on one rare occasion when I questioned her, as I decanted foam from a blender of whisky sours in the kitchen of 53-28. It was the Fourth of July, 1982, and Brian had ferried Mary in from Brooklyn, and I had just returned from Africa, where I had touched, near dawn, with undisguised wonder, a woman whose image no distance could dispel. When my left forefinger brushed her right breast, when the shirr of that touch speared my skull, one lobe knew instantly that I had met my bride; the other, that I would never marry.

"But Aunt Mary, it's been so long," I leered, tapping my glass.

Here in Ohio, at the end of Mary's century, all the intervening years having passed in an instant, Heisenberg taps a finger on her teacup.

"Aunt Mary, I've got to go teach."

"Of course, son," Mary says, squinting up at a face she knows or doesn't. "You're off now; I'll be grand. Do you get more money to teach college boys? Less? You're joking. Ah son, don't worry about me."

What theories could explain Aunt Mary's zigzagging? In the year Einstein first read *Faust*, she crossed the ocean. Her nuptials spirited her to Long Island just as the Grand Mufti's Fatwa endorsed consensual contraception, and her child was born the very month the Bronx-Whitestone Bridge linked two bleak cornices. She returned to her parents' Brooklyn flat on the second anniversary of Hart Crane's death, and her move to 53-28 with her widowed mother occurred the day Walter O'Malley told the *Daily News*, "If they have to be the Flushing Dodgers, they might as well be the Los Angeles Dodgers." Then back to Brooklyn on Kennedy's inauguration, and finally, after my mother's death, she was whisked off with all her kit stuffed into the trunk of her nephew's Taurus to some region beyond time and story.

But Deirdre, her fatherless daughter whose name means Sorrow, aspired to the absolute, craved certainty like salt. Catechized by a family that yo-yoed between skyscraper-awe and piety toward some Hibernian utopia, Deirdre could barely approximate who was above ground and who below. The only certainties were soup, and coins plumbed from purses on nightstands; and men—their shoulderly angles, bourbon and sedans, the hatchets buried in their throats. When she turned sixteen, the beaus who'd fox-trotted her cousins came for her. Deirdre was sure of their doorbell ring, the jangle of their pockets. How easy to churn them; she could draft lust the way a child dials Etch-A-Sketch. A glance, and their pulse quickened. Glare, and they veered off. The fact that men dodged, simpered, or scrammed didn't daunt her. They remained constant as soup, as purses. At seventeen, when the flash of Zeroes over Pearl Harbor blinded her guardians, she shimmied out of their grasp and fled across the river to New Jersey. It wasn't one of the dance-hall dandies who stole her, but a shy boy from Cathedral Prep, a character from the myth I tell my students, the story of Deirdre's name.

In Ulster, millennia before McCann and Martin sowed teeth into each other's flesh, a warrior's widow gave birth to a girl and named her "Sorrow," appealing to King Conchobor for protection. Presented with an infant, the king's eyes gleamed with a design that no woeful prophecy could deter: he'd raise the girl in secret, closeted in the usual fairy-tale minaret, where she'd see no face but his, hear only his voice. Season by season, Deirdre seemed to grow in devotion to the king, who taught her names of stars and essences, elk dances and spells, chariot-fighting and

5

ogham mathematics. "Sorrow," he'd simper, locking her gaze and guiding her slim fingers to his wrist. Then one winter morning, Deirdre glimpsed from her window a young peasant, and that night she endured dreams of ravens diving toward bloodstained snow. How feeble the king seemed now, how banal his lessons compared to this blossoming of exotic faces and bodies, visions that filled her with an ineluctable power. When the next man passed by—a nobleman on horseback—Deirdre didn't just dream, she gave chase.

"What's your name, handsome?" Deirdre asked.

"Niall, first born son of Usnach," the nobleman said, keeping the horse's flanks to the young siren.

"Will you take me, Niall?" Deirdre asked.

"The king's Sorrow?" said Niall. "A made-to-order bride, adopted from scratch? Not a chance. Easier to filch his crown than his clone."

"Then I'll shame you," said Deirdre, stripping off her gown.

She wondered herself where she'd learned that, since stoking lust hadn't been on Conchobor's curriculum. But no education is soporific enough to keep certain kinds of knowledge from Sorrow.

All over Ireland the lovers wandered, even as far as Scotland, taking refuge at Usnach's castle, where Deirdre bore a girl, and was happy, though never able completely to forget her fear. As for the king, rage sharpened his cunning. Promising amnesty, his spies coaxed the fugitives back to Ulster, where the king murdered Niall and his brothers, fulfilling the dream of bloody snow. Conchobor had a baby girl again. As they approached her familiar prison, Deirdre screamed and split her own skull with a spear.

Was this the doppelgänger ensorcelling Deirdre Martin, the certainty she envisioned, tried to grasp? She had her own String Theory, webbing past and future; but the others above ground— grandfather, mother, cousins, lover—plied their roles from the ancient script.

On cue, Francis McCann marched across the bridge to retrieve his charge. Reinstalled in her grandparents' flat, Deirdre carried in her body a rune of certainty's helix: an infant. McCann raged; her cousins hemmed in, their ululations giving grief a skin. But Deirdre would not sway, would not turn back as Mary Martin had been turned. Nor would she split her own skull with a spear. Instead, she locked herself in the bathroom and wedged a chair against the pounding that grew frantic when her moans ceased with a thud and a crash of shattering glass. When they broke through, her cousins found her naked on the linoleum, awash in blood, the mirror sharded, a coat hanger lodged in her womb.

But she did not die, and when she fled again at the age of twenty-two, it was under a shield even her grandfather could not dent, marrying a man to double McCann's rage, a pock-faced Italian with a split-level in Bayside. Soon, her husband unleashed the savagery that Mary Martin feared, flashing Deirdre's brain with blows until she went snow-blank. But still she would not die, raised three living daughters, found work in a flower shop, still bent on her own certainty, charting quarks with bifocals.

When I last saw Deirdre, one summer day on the patio of 53-28 two years before her death, she was already legend: her arms scaly, her hair a hag's nest. Her cousins called her *caution* and spooned the story under my night lamp.

Though I didn't speak to her then, I wonder what I'd say now that she's found certainty. "Only when all are dead is anyone certain," I might say; but that sounds like a Greek chorus. "Let the dead and the living join hands," I'd try; but Deirdre might roll her bloodshot eyes, hearing another crib of the motherly dogma that drove her to flee. Perhaps I wouldn't speak, would pass her unkempt shade, dreading the sisters' caution. Instead, I return to earth, to Ohio, where I stop in Mary's room, find her asleep.

"Is it safe now, Aunt Mary, can I tell?"

"Ah, son, you're back now." Not asleep at all. "Grand. I've been ringing this blessed bell for eons. Nobody comes. Not a soul. I'd like a bit of soup."

"You have to press the button. See, like this. Aunt Mary, listen. Do you remember Deirdre? What was Deirdre like? Tell me about your daughter."

"Ah Deirdre, son, Deirdre was a caution. I took her to Radio City, to the show, with your mother and Betty and Kay, to the Rockettes, do you remember the dancers, son? Gorgeous, they were, and Radio City all lit up and the men in fancy suits, and there she was, Deirdre, the scamp, she let go my hand and skipped down the aisle to join the dancing girls. Imagine. Long gone, she is, long gone. What's that fuzz on your face?"

Even in Ohio, Mary and I hum in the weft of the orbits Deirdre set in motion—doubling above, below: mothers, cousins, daughters, fathers, husbands; and at the gyre's vortex, an empty purse.

2.

WAVE & PARTICLE

God keep me from knowledge of myself.
—Rachel Korn

Mary may exist in the myth-wave, but on Sundays, when I wheel her out of the nursing home, pack her into my car, and drive the few blocks to my apartment, she feels like a weighty particle. She is the joint's ache, what can't be hugged, what can't vault out of herself or melt into the crazy quilt's soft warmth. When I touch her doughy wrist, I feel the origin of the tear between myth and time, wave and particle, as in the buckle of a root-stressed sidewalk. She jolts, wails "Ma!" and I lift her by the armpits, hugging her bulbous torso, and struggle around the coffee table, through the foyer, into the bathroom, where I unfiddle her nylons and peel the viscous panties. I dab her stout thighs with a nest of Kleenex, and mop a trail through the grottiness of Mary Martin, then we waltz to the couch, and I plop her down and unstop a half-bucket of Dewars to water my parched cells. And a thimbleful to quicken Mary's nerves, what-

9

ever wave they dream in. In what's called *me*, in what's called *her*, that potion is deadening, livening right now. God grant we don't outlive ourselves, and a safe journey.

Inside Mary Martin there is still a myth she wakens from, dangling from any of its tines: posing at a booth in Schraft's with her mother and sisters flaunting pillbox Easter hats; Mary eyes the bassinet of salt sticks; the Times Square neon news-ticker undulates DUNKIRK. Then she dives into sleep, reemerges in 1917 palming a shilling at the counter of McCray's Tobacconist and Hairdresser on Merchants Quay. She's seventeen: the Brits, the blackened husks of buildings, the wailing mothers crowd just beyond her ken in a future she escaped; but her young breasts smelling of loam and soap, her calves matted with fine hair—they are waiting to embody dream: What should she buy? She wakes on a couch in her nephew's living room in Ohio; she screams "Ma!" in a senility so perfect it floods the brain, braiding wave and particle.

But like anything else, senility requires toil. In my forties, my waist softening despite drill and starvation, I can only imagine the effort it must take Mary Martin, without stationary bike or vim pills, to perfect memory. Once sleep was her praxis, and she thrashed nightly on the swayback palette of her Brooklyn flat; but no matter how hard she labored to make dream and time cohere, when she woke up, she was always sealed in that sixty- or seventy-or eighty-or ninety-year-old body. Sunlight filtered through the lace over the dresser. She gripped the coverlet and breathed, while the sepia dream dissolved. Years of spindling rounds at Borough Hall, pursefuls of quarters pushed through Automat slots, wave after wave of Welkian bubbles, monthly Rosary Society bus trips to the Cloisters, and always the nightly phone call from Queens finally induced in Mary such a state that she was able to unify the fields while still awake, to slip out of her flat, past the thrice-locked door, to glide through decades and continents without so much as twitching an eye.

Now her discipline is so keen that she *is* the myth, the wave, the waking particle and dream. But all I hear at my desk, as I stare out the window at a shivering oak, is a lick of sibilance burbling from unguessed depths. It sounds like this:

Son, do you remember the time, the time it is, do you remember, son, the time and is it this, the time that you remember? Do you remember that? Son, do you like to drive? Do you drive, son? It's gorgeous, the drive to Hempstead, the long drive. I'm fine, son, I'm grand so, and I'm fine, your mother's gone, gone now, and I wasn't allowed out without her, on dates even, I wasn't allowed.

3.

FIFTY GRAND

*"What do you think about, Jack, when you can't sleep?" I said.
"Oh, I worry," Jack says. "I worry about property I got up in the
Bronx, I worry about property I got in Florida. I worry about the
kids. I worry about the wife . . . . I got some stocks and I worry
about them."*

—Ernest Hemingway

"She's calling *me* now." My brother's voice in the phone, barking into mid-nap, Ohio, a week after I'd moved here in 1994. "She wants to know where the parents are. Can she move in with them."

"Hello, Brian."

"What—were you asleep?"

"No. Working. Who's calling you?"

"Who do you think, Gomer? Aunt Mary."

"What did you say?"

"I reminded her about the parents' funerals."

"And?"

"She didn't miss a beat. Talked about the cold cuts at Pet's wake. Looks like she'll be moving in with them soon enough. Maybe that's what she meant."

"And in the meantime?"

"I don't know. We've got to do something."

"Like what?"

"Like Kevorkian."

"Well, at least we can afford him."

And this was and remains waking fact, though shrouded in drowsy jokes. In 1990, when my father could no longer pretend to walk, his holster traded for a colostomy bag, my parents sold 53-28, which they had bought in 1957 for eleven grand, for one-hundred-ninety-seven-thousand-five-hundred dollars. The real-estate tsunami bore them beyond Queens, across the river and into the lap of Mr. Bosco Minihan, comptroller of Mirror Lake Retirement Home, Livingstone, New Jersey.

Polo-shirted, cheeks glossy with the good life, Bosco Minihan cakewalked around his glass-topped desk and plucked my father's hand from his tin walker.

"Mr. and Mrs. *Brady*," he said, welcoming shipwrecks. Turning to me, his brow uncreased, "You must be Phil Junior."

And he shook my hand on the fact that we, at least, would live, and led us all through the mauve corridors, navigating the course of carts and wheelchairs, his steps like grace notes around my father's turgid march. We inched past sailboats braving the whitecaps, dogs at cards, boxers facing off. At the arched atrium of the dining room, we halted to view a quarter-acre of china and chandeliers, a hundred tables draped with linen, creased sharply. In the paneled library, we cooed at the overstuffed chairs and banker's lamps. Minihan gestured toward mahogany bookshelves twinkling with gilt titles.

"We've done Mirror Lake in the old style," he said, "like the big houses in the Poconos—you remember Fred Waring's resort, don't you, Phil?"

Despite the bluster, it was impossible to forget that under the shrink-wrap of a four-star resort was a working hospital: nurse's stations, guardrails, emergency buzzers. For an entrance fee of a hundred thousand dollars per, plus direct deposit *in perpetua* of pension and social security, Bosco opened heaven's vestibule to offer permanent relief from earthly obligations.

But decamping from Flushing was harder than Mr. Minihan made it seem. It was not the row house—the closets crammed with how-to books, balls of string, baseball gloves, kneepads, garden hoses and trophies, each nook tallowed with memories, nor was it the fact that 53-28 had guarded its own secret: increasing in value the way a redwood pads rings. It was not the parish, which had shifted beneath them as Brooklyn had once shifted, leaving Bronco Pucerelli the last English-speaking neighbor on the block, and it was not my mother's career, which had prospered beyond ambition until she became Dr. Rosenshein's personal assistant—the Rasputin of Special Ed. It was the rivers and highways that threatened to separate Pet from Aunt Mary, because what bound these sisters was no love a boy could fathom, a bond the middle sisters, Betty and Kay, slipped. Even Mary's daughter and her three granddaughters broke free, and after Deirdre's death, her children scorned their grandmother like some skirted Lear. But not Pet. Every evening after dinner, from the Cuban Missile Crisis through Iran-Contra, she mounted the stairs to call Aunt Mary for the prescribed minutes and the benediction. And the finish was always the same.

"Phil's yelling up, Dear," Pet would say, "I have to go."

And God forbid she miss a day.

"If I don't call, she sulks," my mother sighed, sinking into her orange chair.

"Why not not call for a week?" I said.

"My God, could you imagine?" And she couldn't.

Something webbed them in another world. But how to decode? How to know what my father's clenched jaw meant; why an aura of bruise flared from his white hair when he raised his glass. Does it still hold, now that my own name is an escape route? Does my brother feel the pull? Will he mount the stairs at the prescribed hour? Maybe as a child I feared Brian would never phone when I slouched in striped boxers in an old-age home. Maybe this was why I pounded his kidneys during commercials. I was afraid that he would never call to ask about my toast.

Yet he does call, from his rented car or hotel room on a sales trip, or from his home in Bucks County, trying to tutor his older brother in the ways of the world. When I tell him I want to buy a house, if only to leverage tenure, I feel his finger, even over the phone, poking my chest.

"Location, location, location," he says.

"What's a good location, near a bar?"

"It's what people think is good. It can change—look at Flushing."

"But I can buy a fixer-upper near campus for next to nothing. And I've had it with bringing Aunt Mary over here to sit on the couch like we're back in 53-28. Let her spit up in a bigger house."

"You don't buy real estate in a ghost town."

"So what do I do with the money?"

"Rent. Buy mutuals. Listen, Batman, don't sign anything without calling me first."

Money, real estate, wave, desire: These do not exist in space. Even location, it appears, does not exist in Ohio, and in this light another question looms: Where did the rest of the cash come from? Sure, my parents reserved a place in Heaven, N.J., with the proceeds of the row house, but there's more. After all the counting there remained an unaccounted-for fifty grand.

A month after the cold-cut funeral, Brian and I slouched at the Sears cherrywood table from 53-28, dwarfed in my brother's dining room, with the detritus of half a century between us, a Jurassic mound glittering with greenstamps, check stubs, communion-breakfast raffle tickets, paper-clip chains tangled in rosary beads, Chesterfield coupons, Nixon-Agnew buttons, ribbon, Claddagh earrings, and rubber erasers. I stuck my arms into the pile and wiggled my fingers.

"Cut the crap," Brian said. "We've got to figure this out."

"Maybe they were sharks after all." My hands finned through the pile. "Maybe they made a killing in the market."

"Nah," Brian said. "It looks like everything was in a money market at five-point-five percent."

"Are we sure we want to know?" I asked.

"What do you mean?"

"Remember how Dad hated Serpico? He wouldn't even watch the movie, made us switch the channel. Maybe he was a bagman."

Brian squeezed his temples.

"Hell, the whole Police Force might have been crooked." I said. "He could have been in on it."

"Except that the parents didn't have any savings until 1974, Kojak; eight years after he retired." Brian flicked through the serrated stubs and, touching fortune with a pencil point, said, "Here. Look. A deposit for fifty thousand dollars."

Could it be that Mary Martin amassed, from her job as cleaning lady, from social security, and from a tiny pension, $50,000? She took the bus to Atlantic City every month, spent a roll of quarters, ate nothing but dry toast between holiday meals at 53-28, always wore the same paisley dress, the same plastic clip-on earrings. Yet there it was: the myth as fact. Fifty grand.

As far as we can make it out, here's what happened. In 1974, when Brooklyn finally ceased to exist as real estate, a raft of ghosts was stranded and something had to be done: Mary had already been mugged twice on Prospect Avenue and burgled so often, her flat was lint-free. Queens was out; Phil Brady would not have Mary back, whinging for Lawrence Welk, when it had taken his last spunk to evict her. A haven was needed for all the refugees who would not give up the thought that Brooklyn was still a viable destination. And who better than the bishop and his church to pry a crosier between sublunary and ideal Brooklyn? The Catholic Church had built a refuge for the cleaning ladies, janitors, and widows, and to pass through the gates, the church required the opposite of Mr. Minihan's fee: proof that the last penny had already been leeched. But Mary Martin, if the myth is to be believed, had been compounding until her Dime Saving Bank passbook grew so unwieldy that she could not squeak through the needle's eye. She signed it all over to her Pet, who would hold her fortune and wheel her through the great doors of Bishop Boardman Apartments as pure as a bride, to be welcomed by a flutter of nuns and the potbellied guard with holster and coke-bottle specs, offering her nightgowned body to the coarse, safe sheets.

The story reached me in 1975 in the dusk of the city where I first lived alone. I slouched against the streaky glass of a green phone booth, staring at a wall of unmortared stone over the backwash of a river, studying the linseed torsos of swans, filthy and lithe. Even through double panes they resisted metamorphosis. The city was Cork: spare-voweled, meaning *swamp*; lesion between earth and water. Cork: a place I found by rocking, back and forth, haunches to knees and palms to rug, in front of the hi-fi at 53-28.

For years I'd rocked, bound by the scratchy bark of Irish LPs, the disks translated into sound, needling grooves through the place where the row house padded value, where my parents kept their secrets and were kept from knowing where the secrets led. I'd rocked, forward toward river, backward toward ebb, forth toward distance, back toward the mysterious bond that had sent Pet upstairs every night to make a call. Finally I was here, phoning home collect, by grace of the capital whose source could not be traced. My call drew Pet up the stairs. I imagined her mounting the taupe carpeted steps as I shivered in a mossy turret by a feather-stroke of water.

I imagine it now, my mother's voice layered over my brother's, over sleep, in Ohio, as I heard it then in Cork, feeling night's vastness brim my eyes.

"Flip. Hello, Flip. I'm upstairs. Your father's asleep. Can you hear me?"

And so she revealed one strand of that bond: how she'd taken charge of Mary's finances and found a place for her on the bishop's raft. But she kept secret the magical amount.

This we are left to unspool, Brian and I, sleeping and waking, living in place and no place, stringing together words, in New York or in open-voweled Ohio, trying by phone, breadth of a hand, to join the double nature, as if we could press the past into a coin: heads, secret; tails, memory. Heads, stone. Tails, water. Heads, grave. Tails, whatever it is that endures.

4.

FIRST FUNERALS

Whichever monkey got Prozac dominated.
—Peter D. Kramer

Character is fate.

—Heraclitus

THE first funerals my brother and I planned were for each other, three Thursdays after Samhain in 1985, before any sister had died, though all but Pet had buried their husbands and commenced squinting into the darkness. But this was America, no Samhain here, only Thanksgiving, when even brooding spirits face horrid traffic. While my father rattled pans in the kitchen, Brian and I schlepped on the Long Island Expressway over the Kosciusko Bridge to collect Aunt Kay on Sterling Place, then over to Mary at Bishop Boardman, then back to Queens, and out again on that nightmare expressway to the Island to snatch Betty from her son's ranch house in Merrick. We sat them in the living room like knickknacks: Mary in her old spot in the parlor wingback and Betty, who'd moved from Flushing after her husband died, bookending Kay on the flowered couch. At night, woozy from Rusty Nails, tryptophan, and football, we crisscrossed again from

Brooklyn to the gullet of the East Island. It was during the last trip with Aunt Betty that Brian and I concocted our funeral plan.

"It's in the air, I tell you," Betty whined, poking Brian's arm. "The bastard sneaks in at night and sprays poison in the air, in the food too. He thinks I don't taste it." She squinched her face and hawked a gob of phlegm on the dashboard.

"Don't take me back, Brian, don't make me go back there."

Brian mopped his hanky on the nickel of spit and said, "Aunt Betty, your son's not trying to kill you." He twisted toward the backseat, risking the press of his suit to pass me a silver flask, and growled, "He may not get the chance."

We didn't murder Aunt Betty but instead propped her on the porch swing next to a dogwood tree and slipped off before our cousin spotted us. As Brian rammed the Cougar into reverse, bisecting the S-curve driveway into a dollarsign, he told me that if he ever got like that, he wanted me to shoot him.

"Me too," I said, but without conviction, knowing that, to him, I might already be halfway there.

The supreme imperative in Brian's life was to be as little like the rest of us as genetics allowed. Since I was closest in age, and since my nightly dinner battles with my father made it clear that genes were bequeathed, Brian concentrated on being unlike me. I liked school, so he refused to read. I sang Clancy tunes, so he rocked to The Stones. My head was as lopsided as an eggplant, so he became the handsomest boy in school. I never dated, so he married, at twenty-one, Pet's spitting image.

As we drove back from the Island through midnight on the deserted highway after depositing Aunt Betty, sipping whisky with an eye out for the police, I considered funerals, genes, my brother, Heraclitus, and Job. Brian and I have inherited two ghosts. Whatever the weather, hardship, serotonin drought, or death, Job is determined to thwart his apparent fate, as Brian is determined to Houdini himself out of Brady-McCann gene cabling. But what about his phone calls to Ohio? The taxi service he ran for relatives? What about his beautiful wife, who looks so much like his mother? And me—with all my meandering, why are my eyes fixed on a blue screen, brooding on Queens?

Character *is* fate. If Brian and I make it as far as senility, one of us will release the burden of memory and, like Mary, let it dissipate into air, synapses clean as polished cutlery. The other, like Betty, will hang on to some twisted root, compelled to reknot connections, refusing to drift, to ripple into being, to move.

Heraclitus and Job continue to sluice down the starlit expressway, passing whisky, promising, brother to brother, a good death. When the day comes when one of us is perfect, the other gnarled into an anguished shape, we'll square off somewhere—on a highway or in a hospital room—pistols drawn. A single shot rings out. Which of us will it be?

5.

A GRAVE OF ONE'S OWN

Good friend for Jesus Sake forbear
to Digg Ye Dust Encloased Heare
Blesse Be Y man Y spares thes stones
And Curst be He Y Moves my Bones
　　　　　　　　—WILLIAM SHAKESPEARE

W<small>HATEVER</small> ethereal shoe box Mary's fortune came from, her three grandchildren never knew. They were schooled by a different skein of facts altogether: their father's fists, a Catholic separation, and the bifurcation of their own identities into Irish and Italian. Once a year, they'd climb the stoop at 53-28 behind Deirdre, huddling around her skirts as she primped through the screen door like exiled royalty. The whole troupe emanated scandal, summed up in the word "divorce." They lived, it was whispered, in a tiny Astoria flat over the flower shop where Deirdre worked.

On Sundays, while the country dervished through the nineteen-sixties, their father, the construction king, would drive his finned Chrysler to Astoria and whisk the three girls to Little Italy for a day with their paternal relations. No whispering here, no murmurs of distant scandal. With its muraled virgins, tribunals of crones, and plate-glass windows shimmering with flake and

21

cream, their Italian heritage was incarnated, frangible. And long after they grew up, maybe they brought their own children to Mulberry for the San Gennaro Festival to see the hoisted saint slathered with dollars. Maybe it was the sight of this icon lumbering on the shoulders of the past that made them decide to unearth their mother's bones.

I sit at my desk, fingering the cream keyboard, stare dumbly at the screen, breathe *bones*, and fog its blue suffocation. I've inhabited this body for an epoch of foibles and have yet to provide for its disposition to the grave. Habitual motion, rocking and traveling and curling back over old routes, feeds dreams of serial rebirth, an illusion the McCanns, surviving exile, could not afford. Finances boggled them—the decimals and bankbooks and social security and the tax jigging around and through it all like a pooka. But they could do high math on their talismans and knickknacks. Letters, scapulars, certificates, chessmen, rosaries—even a velvet purse containing a few grains of Ulster soil—all were ordered in brilliant equations that came to the right answer. So too would their bodies, at the last hour, need precise inventory.

Who would perform the accounting? Who else but the sister who'd climbed the stairs each night and finagled the apartment from Bishop Boardman? Without campaigning, Pet found herself elected chief mourner of the future. In 1957, as if to establish that Queens would be the limit of the McCann migration, she acquired from Flushing cemetery adjacent plots sufficient to accommodate the four sisters and their three remaining husbands. Space being finite, especially in Queens, there were no guest rooms. She chose a single granite headstone to be inscribed with seven names and dates; the contract and deed to plots 7-13 in Lot 12, Section 4, 3rd Division lay in the bottom drawer of the dining room cabinet, awaiting need.

But the descending order went topsy-turvy in 1976, when Deirdre was diagnosed with ovarian cancer and died within a month. The news reached me in the same green phone booth where I'd heard the story of Mary's fortune, wafting from a past as distant as the prophecy of Deirdre's name. At the funeral, Pet said, Mary had seemed dazed, bereft of words and tears, and I imagined her vacant face staring into a future flensed of syntax. There'd been no time, no one was prepared for such a thing. A terrible shame, and the children all so young, the eldest just sixteen.

Deirdre's name graced no parish rolls, so Pet had interceded for a Mass at St. Kevin's and arranged to bury her in Mary's place. I imagined Pet rummaging through the bottom drawer for the deed in its manila sleeve, hovering while the notary stamped the changes—Mary's name struck out, replaced with her daughter's. Peering out at the River Lee and the Mardyke Bar, with its swan-head-painted signpost, I followed my mother as she climbed the pebbly steps and pinched the shamrock knocker on the rectory door, begging a Mass from Monsignor Barry, calling at the funeral home whose card she'd taken from the old priest's palsied hand, and shepherding her elder sister back to the Brooklyn flat her efforts had secured two years before.

For eight years after Deirdre's funeral, while I drifted from Queens to Ireland to Africa, Deirdre's three girls blossomed into womanhood, married, and started families of their own, and Deirdre festered in her borrowed grave, rooting in their minds, until finally, when the site was opened again for Kay's husband, Terry Dolan, they could stand it no longer. They had to claim her bones from a place they did not believe was real, a place they could understand no better than I understood my mother's nightly phone calls to Aunt Mary. So they conceived a plan and sent a letter addressed to their grandmother and her sisters.

I have this letter, typed on yellowing unheaded stationery marked by eraser burns, and I have just read it again for the hundredth time, thinking of my cousins buttoning their Easter coats for their mother's funeral. I entered it word for word on the screen, my own small square of mortgaged future. I read and reread how my cousins wanted their mother back, were prepared to take the body, to exhume it, though eight years had passed. They had waited, suffered, finally it was too much—going back to the grave, seeing the earth opened again at Uncle Terry's funeral. They needed to venerate Deirdre in their own, separate place, so that they could be certain of one sliver of earth.

But I have deleted my cousins' words. Perhaps I betray them again. Maybe, like Pet, I have taken over a responsibility best left to others. "Only when all are dead is anyone certain," I wrote, parroting Sophocles. But all are never dead. Another strand of the web frays, another living body rises to haunt. Here in Ohio, in a wet, freezing spring, I look out at the bare trunk of an oak and, like my cousins, I crave Deirdre's certainty. Let no voice or image intervene. Let the past unfold—exact, encompassing. I would reject any version which did not render each joint and vein, each contour of the face, each strand of hair, if resurrection could redeem the gargantuan relic. But it can't. My cousins' words are smudged by many hands; this is what they say to me, unmoored from time.

We are the invisible, disinherited by our blood, shamed and gawked at in Easter suits. Our father you have disowned, our mother taken. We write because we cannot speak. We are figments to you. You will not unearth our heart's desire. But we live, we are here, will not be transposed. We want only and exactly what you want: to cleave. Had we the strength to speak in any other way, we would. We do not want to lie in the earth alone. We will not be divided from our lives. We have planned. We have bought a plot at Mount St. Mary Cemetery and we will have our mother's body. Please understand this is not easy. We want her glorified, but at least we must embrace her beloved frame once before eternity begins. At Uncle Terry's funeral, the pain rushed over us. Overwhelmed. We cannot bear not to redeem, take leave of. Her name will be erased and reinscribed. We hope you will respect. This we must do.

Sincerely,
Bridget, Maureen, and Ellen

I was not the recipient of the grandchildren's letter whose words I ghost here. Its first incarnation was franked on March 4th, 1982, an afternoon I spent drinking palm wine in the savanna of Katanga. Four copies were sent, each addressed to all the sisters. There was, to my knowledge, only one written response, from Kay's only son, whose father had just joined Deirdre in the grave. Knowing Terry Dolan, Jr., with his psoriasis, his comb-over, his swollen forearms and caved-in chest, I could hardly believe he had been a golden child. But I've seen the snapshots: a blonde boy with saucer eyes and Hollywood curls. And I have a surreal memory of a summer afternoon in the backyard of 53-28, Terry's slender legs meandering up from the rubber play-pool toward plaid trunks. He never married, slept in the bunk his parents had rigged in the foyer in their rent-fixed flat, with a fetid quilt and plastic votive font above the dresser. When his turn came, Terry claimed his sinecure in special education.

I have his letter too in the olive footlocker I have inherited. He told the granddaughters they'd need a new undertaker, new gravediggers, a new sandblaster, a new deed, low-life clerks, and a harebrained curate. "I find it sad," he wrote, "when you say that 'we will have my mother's body removed from its present grave site to this new grave site. In this way, both Mom and us are assured of an eternity with the ones we loved most dearly.' I say that I am sad because an eternity in a hole in the ground is a terrifying thought." He hammered on the message of Easter, reminding them that while they mulled their plans to exhume and rebury their mother, his father's gravestone remained uninscribed, the stonecutters waiting to see if Deirdre's name was to be effaced. "Have you no consideration for the living?" he thundered.

Once Terry Dolan found his voice, there was no stopping him. Letter after letter he sent, straight from the tradition of cursing that could scald feathers at a hundred paces, each signed, "Your cousin in Christ," with copies to everyone this side of the Styx.

Speaking these letters aloud in my hollow voice, decades off, I can see why they were all too much for the grandchildren. Terry had them on all counts: defacing, undertaking, and heresy. So they gave up. What must they have felt, receiving instead of their mother's body these words, urgent and purposeful? Cursed?

Deirdre remained in her borrowed plot, the plot bought for Mary and surrendered to her unlucky daughter, while the dirt turnstile grunted to admit Kay, and Betty, and her husband Tom. By the time Phil and Anne Brady died in 1994, the feud had gone cold and the grave was almost forgotten; I was in transit from California to Ohio, and my brother had long ago left Queens, both of us flailing in midlife, so we buried my parents only months apart in a new grave near the Philadelphia suburb where Brian and his family lived. Only Mary was left aboveground, like the poor crippled boy who couldn't follow the Pied Piper into the cave.

She was still puttering in her Bishop Boardman apartment when my parents died, though she'd been declining for years and was kept there only because Pet paid the bills, did the shopping, and made her nightly phone calls. As for me—I had just arrived in Ohio, my ears still ringing from my brother's first phone call, invoking Kevorkian. Inevitably, he called again.

"You awake, Gilligan?"

"Hello, Brian."

"I'm getting calls from nuns now. Sister Mercedes. They name them after cars these days. They say they don't have the facilities to keep Aunt Mary any longer. What facilities does she need besides a toaster?"

"Well, I guess you have to do something quick," I said.

"Whaddaya mean, *me*?"

"Can't you take her for a while?"

"Christ, no."

"Why not? You said she doesn't need much. Mary got kicked out of 53-28 in the first place because you were born, and she's never had a day's luck since. Me neither, come to think of it."

"Hey, we got a dog. Things are nuts enough around here. What about you doing something for a change, instead of fucking off missing all the funerals. That way you'll bank some of them indulgences for when you're sitting in an old-age hole with racing stripes—and it'll be sooner than you think, with all your boozing. Who do you think's going to pick your bony ass off the floor? My kids? It's your turn now." I'd covered the mouthpiece and lit a cigarette, and Brian didn't miss a beat.

"And you smoke. Just great. I hope you've taken care of that will like I told you. I ain't going through this paperwork again."

"Thanks. When I croak I want you to go to a little trouble."

"Try to hold out at least till we get Aunt Mary settled. Got any ideas?"

"Well," I chanced, feeling the noose tighten, "what about her grandkids."

"Who?"

"Don't you remember—Deirdre's kids—the big fight about the grave. They must still be alive."

"I saw them years ago at Uncle Terry's funeral. Mary didn't even know who they were. I hardly knew them myself."

"Maybe you could work with them. They might want to take in their grandmother."

"After all these years—you kidding?"

"If anyone can charm them, you can."

"Yeah, I'll write a poem."

I groaned out of bed and padded into my office, thinking of Deirdre's daughters' last words.

April 16, 1983

We reached out to you in our need, you spewed back venom. If these are your mother's words, and your aunts, then who are we? We have canceled our plans. We will not redeem, take leave. As you insinuate, the price is too high. This will be the last communication between us.

Your cousins,

Bridget, Maureen, and Ellen

I lit another smoke and flopped down on the couch, eyeing the Styrofoam peanuts and bubble wrap, exhaling a deep drag to Brian's intention of finding the lost grandchildren. He did track them down, somehow, by phone book or credit check or Internet or private eye, and arranged for a summit in her Bishop Boardman flat to decide the fate of Mary Martin, grandmother, aunt, eternal spider, last stop on the McCann line. And what a meeting it must have been. Brian with his cashmere and swagger, and the three granddaughters, seated on the flowered couch with Aunt Mary, sizing him up as he strode across the room and gripped each of their hands, then bent to Aunt Mary to kiss her forehead.

"Hey, Aunt Mary, howyadoin," he'd have said. And the granddaughters—the rightful heirs to this dwindling legacy—seeing Mary's face turned upward, seeing her raise her arms like a slo-mo ref calling a touchdown, they'd have stiffened, glaring across Mary's dappled coffee table at this groomed stranger.

"Nobody ever talked to me like that," Brian fumed the next day on the phone. "I couldn't believe it. I think even Mary was scared."

"I'm sure they're just pissed off about the grave, and that was so long ago. They want to take care of their grandmother, don't they?"

"Like hell. When they found out about the money. . . ."

"You *told* them?" I swept off the blankets.

"They should know. Anyway, it'll be smoked up in the first year. Do you have any idea what nursing homes cost? Remember Mirror Lake?"

"But don't you think they might feel a bit slighted, being left out of the picture so long?"

"What picture? We didn't even know the whole story till Pet died."

"But you haven't read these letters. There was a lot of bad blood between them and Terry. They wanted to dig up Deirdre and bury her somewhere else."

"What letters?"

"I've got a metal box here—the whole lousy history."

"And this is how you spend your day? Reading dead people's mail?"

"It's quite a tale," I said.

"To you everything's a tale. That's the problem. You weren't even there. You were off playing Stanley and Leprechaun. What do you know about it?"

"I know enough to know that the grandkids think they got dealt out. Now cash is on the table, what are they going to do?"

"They don't want her, Bullwinkle. When I brought it up, they said, 'What has our grandmother ever done for us?' It was a soap opera. A lot of fucking screaming. I'm telling you, I had to look down to make sure I still had a dick."

So that is how it happens that I sit in an apartment in Ohio, staring at a rain-slicked tree trunk, my aunt muttering on the couch. And they—the abandoned grandchildren—they wait for the time to play their part, when Mary will be ready for them, when they can claim her body.

But if Brian and I have failed to uncoil fate, at least we have planned for one frayed thread, the sister left behind long after the others were sprinkled with the soil they had kept in velvet purses. If Mary ever dies, Szabo and Sons Funeral Home will dispatch her by hearse three hundred ninety six miles along Route 80, over the George Washington Bridge, down the Cross-Bronx Expressway, over the Throgs Neck to Clearview, right on

Northern, left on Crockeron, right on 35th, left on 162nd, to Flushing Cemetery, in sea wind, and there, without prayer or mourner, deposit Mary in my mother's place in the plot once battled over, where Mary's daughter lies.

If I live to see that day, I will walk out onto the rutted streets of this mid-Western ghost town and exhale cigarette smoke, gathering in my arms the shapes curling upward, caressing the specters of the McCann girls in their far-flung plots—trying to hold them, impossibly, for just a moment.

No. Prayers are not enough, and finally no distance can be abided, as my cousins have taught. I will not grieve for smoke. In our separate cars, from separate lives, Brian and I will take one more trip, on highways and boulevards, through horrid traffic, to converge on that one-hearse highway funeral procession. To atone for revising our parents' final plans, we will attend as Mary is buried in Pet's grave. Then, together, we will lay a parcel of letters on the fresh-turned soil, and the long, perfect forgetting can begin.

PART TWO

BARD & GODDESS

I am a farmer so that my son can be a lawyer so that my grandson can be a poet.

—Thomas Jefferson

6.

RAGE, GODDESS

My work is all stamped down into the sultry mud.

—W. B. YEATS

My cousins raged, voiceless, invisible; and my parents are invisible, beyond. How can I delve into the time before? Can this old woman asleep on my couch be the Muse? No wonder Homer went blind squinting at her. No wonder "Rage" was the first word of his first poem. "Rage, Goddess," he began, shaking her awake. Aunt Mary, one sorry deity. What would she intone? "Sing the rage of Francis McCann, miner, Ulster Taig?" He was not murderous, exactly; there were no countless heroes dealt to the house of death, only his own shade skulking at the pit mouth. No sleek ships set forth on the wine-dark sea, only four whelps and a dowdy wife to feed. Still, I'd like to versify, hear a Goddess keen into the gin-soaked night.

Why not? I'm failing solo. I can't spindle the past out of Aunt Mary. Together we scaled this afternoon with maudlin tunes, dancing from window to couch, bobbing to her Delphic cackles,

33

which can't traverse a century or an ocean to raise the stooped specter of that coal-breaker Francis McCann. We're no Bard and Goddess, only his daughter and grandson warbling ditties, and as for dancing, together we make a mirror-cracking beast.

Aunt Mary's snoring now, and McCann's farther off, his mouth a coal seam. So, Goddess, if you're out there, start us off. Belch open the Armagh hill fields crossed with feuds, a century ago, underneath the drumlin furze. Sing us a man alive again, here in Ohio. Use this cracked voice. Tunnel me down, let rage pass through bones and worms. Scrub death off. Forge light. Please? For a drink? A prayer? A wreath of wind-torn clouds? That's all I have to offer, sealed off from the past. Well, not quite all. There's Mary, your familiar, last spasm of the lust that drove Francis McCann to heave under horsehair blankets, one October Saturday night in 1900, and mount his wife Sarah, née Heaney, youngest of eleven. Were you there, Goddess, stiffening the embers? Samhain night, the shadows flush with ghosts.

"The fire, the fire," Aunt Mary chanted almost a century later, up from the couch. "What a nice fire," as we swayed, her eyes wide with delight, my left hand clamped to her back, my right waving a martini big as a lampshade, the two of us dancing on the roiling carpet, singing, "Oh the fire's gorgeous."

Where did she learn this pleasure, this swaying? Something almost eternal made Mary yelp "fire" tonight, her violet hands flaming in my palms. If a coal-smeared Goddess gestated this rheumy dance, maybe she kindled in McCann's skull, as it receded from the infinite, a small flame shaped in queenly profile. Maybe from the moment of Mary's conception McCann followed that gleam underground, beneath the pleats and buckles of the rage-torn surface of Ulster, where, sealed off from sky, it became his substitute for clouds, drink, and prayer. Over the years, soot cooled the flame until his blood was mercury-thick. And in his palm each week, a coin, always etched with the same head. He might have thought it the flaming Goddess's profile. All he knew of the future: a doll-small pillar of coins. To live, he relinquished a ha'penny for minerals at the pub, six shillings for milk and spuds, five pennies to be frittered away by the wife. Nothing for church.

A pillar of coins rose in his blood, and when their taste soured, they began to stamp his sleep's mud: faint veins of bridges, towers, boulevards, machines. Even in sleep he remained clenched. No wafting o'er the sea, no softening tunes. In rage and blindness, lacking sky, he traced sulfurous lines into a design.

What young man, sealed off from sight and from himself, doesn't start this way? In 1975, when I first flew over Ireland's dawn, my stomach fluttering, what had brought me but a glimpse of flame? I was there to reclaim Francis McCann's life as if I were the last coin under his thumb. Such was the power he conceived and provides still as correspondent on this Heraclitian screen, where I test margins as his kerosene lamp searched nooks in the black mine. But if McCann provided coins, my own design was not to return to a place I'd never been but to smash all the designs that had made me. Hopeless, of course. I was blind then too, tracing in the endless desert of childhood sounds grooved from LPs: the Clancy Brothers & Tommy Makem, Paddy Noonan's Irish Party, John McCormack. I crouched in front of the cabinet hi-fi and rocked, the warped disks crackling.

Emigrating backwards, I wasn't aiming toward an afternoon in a mid-Western ghost town capering with a senile muse; I wanted to make myth of the time before Queens. But it was no Promised Land I arrived in. I'd packed light, but couldn't help but heft the jet disk of a heart that mistook rocking for traveling, scratchy recordings for the whisper of a Goddess's voice. The truth is, I could no more escape Queens, when all was said and done, than McCann could escape hell. After slaving in mine shafts, McCann arrived in Brooklyn and ignored the sky, the bridges, and the dizzying towers, and descended the subway stairs, his fingers rhyming the enameled banister. In a soot-black uniform, screwed into the conductor's cab of a subway car, he squinted like Homer through a streaked pane, rasping "Nostrand Avenue" into the microphone. I see his fingers as he trundled beneath Brooklyn, prodding the spikes of his cap's badge, as if testing which prong inexplicably blipped its signal back, through metal, steam, over unimaginable water, through Armagh's soot, to the tunnel he'd spent his last shilling to escape.

On Sundays, McCann yanked his family down with him, doling out nickels to his five ducklings, fussed up in their Mass clothes for a fête in Hades. But the coins were not for the ferryman to pluck from eyelids (this would require, as there were ten eyes, twice the expense) but to fit into a turnstile slot thin as a wink. First Sarah, bibbed in twill and flax, plugged her nickel and pressed her fecund belly to the slab and turned. Then Mary placed her hands on the altar wood and pushed. Then Betty lifted her chin and arms, wading as if through brackish water. Then Kay dropped the nickel in the luck-pond and touched the wood cross with her giggly throat. And finally Pet, her face squinched up, placed her votive nickel on the grill and ducked under. So they entered the underworld, shivering with the knowledge that the next bulge of light, the next thunder, quickening screech of brakes, the next steam-spurt expressed from unseen valves, was the visible motility of their father's rage, which had always been sovereign but never, before America, incarnate.

They went underground on Sundays to bear witness as they had never witnessed in Armagh, where hill-grass blanketed the truth. If McCann had brought them to America to escape, the price was this: entering the car and sitting stiff-backed on the faux horsehair cushions, feeling the pull shift them westward, release them back into each other's flanks; hearing the engine clear its throat and speak in their father's amplified Ulsterese, "Nostrand next."

And years later, just as McCann had dressed his family for excursions through his personal Cocytus, so my parents followed his paint-by-number design, spraying down my cowlick and buttoning my brother's butchy togs to spank us from Mass into the black Dodge over the Van Wyck Expressway to Idlewild. They made the weekly pilgrimage to the airport not to fly but to press noses against church-tall windows and watch the Boeings take off. Was this more tomfoolery, Goddessimmo? Instead of subway cars, arched airport corridors; instead of steam, vapor. And when finally I took off in one of the planes I'd ogled as a child, touching down at Shannon and squeezing through customs and striding for the first time into the country Francis McCann had hoarded coins to escape, I could see, after all, nothing.

Just as the grooves of McCann's design spiraled downward to the subway, at first my tunnel vision registered only green telephone booths, palm trees, corbelled stone huts—all shrunken to the toy detritus that I'd tweezed, a child, with tiny cranes from plastic cases in the airport tourist shop. But one day all that changed. After hitching to Cork and taking digs and hiking fields past the Mardyke through the twisting lanes of Sunday's Well to Gurranabraher and standing over the spread of the marshy burg crowing refrains I'd rocked into memory in front of the hi-fi, and after weeks of swatting *The Course of Irish History* and *Ireland Since the Famine* and *Irish Poets in English* (The Thomas Davis Lectures) and *The Golden Treasury of Irish Poetry* at one of the desks bolted in strict rows in the Aula Maxima under the curdling portraits of O'Connell, Hyde, Emmett, and Parnell, and after enduring lectures by the crow-robed poets and historians who delivered their orations not to the second-arts candidates crammed in tiers but to the venerable portraits themselves, and after drinking myself broke in student dives from the *Idle Buachaill* to the Western Star, one Sunday afternoon I found myself wandering MacCurtain Street in T-shirt and smeared London Fog, finally staring at something I understood.

"Help Wanted," the crayoned sign read, taped to a shop door.

Even more intriguing was the life-sized mural decaled on plate glass, the huge nap and patina of Captain America, shooting off spangles from his Technicolor cape. I was so homesick, I started talking to him, asking what he made of it, these alleys and spires and birds strafing the Lee, the sky grimy as a subway and the bitter past washing over the crowds on Patrick's Street with their heads so bowed my adam's apple bobbed over a sea of caps and scarves. For answer, this Marvel hero thrust open the door with mantled fist and winked me in. I stepped right through and, though tinged with none of his masculine pith, I spoke in the only voice that could plausibly be his, so I was hired on the spot.

I was far too important to work in the front dining room. This I gathered from the owner—a new breed, *Chara* businessman—wasp-waisted, mustachioed, with a coif that curlicued behind dainty ears. Small as he was, he led me by the elbow while my head swiveled on its stalk.

"But so, you're a Yank, you'll understand all this," he said, passing his hand over the puzzle of tiles, plastic tables festooned with picnic napkins—the way the Russian bumpkin in *Heart of Darkness* passed over the spiked skulls surrounding Kurtz's stronghold.

He guided me through the kitchen, with its veneer of chrome barely hiding the ulcerated pipes. Cardboard soaked up the swill; the walls were splashed red and blue; the stanchions were striped like barbers' poles. My boss saluted the chips man—a great bearded slump—and the burger man, who wheezed a tubercular, "Halloo, yah," as we made our way through the trashy bazaar to the last station: the great double zinc tub of the kitchen sink.

There I was left to work for the head muck-maker, Finbar, whose jet eyes and olive skin lent credence to the legend that sailors from the wrecked Armada swam into the arms of Munster women. Finbar, the pizza chef upon whose rhymes, it was said, an Armada of women had been wrecked.

This was work, where McCann's design had been forged, performed with forearms, raw mitts, nagging muscles. McCann's work: blindness, a searing in the branches of the back. Mine: blindness, a searing in the branches of the back. His: soot. Mine: the dreck of plates. His: the harrowing of earth, feeling its refusal to be known. Mine: the intimacy of strangers—which ones slobbered meat, who disdained onions, who slashed half-baked notions in the grease. His: a lifetime underneath the city his design had brought him to. Mine: an epiphany on MacCurtain Street. And if I drifted, forgetting for a moment that without the bang of tin and splash of water the Captain's cape would peel, Finbar would peer around the corner, arching his black eyebrows, and shout, "You're doing fook all back here."

In Cork, even curses thrilled. That they would speak to me at all in this watery tongue, foisted by botched designs dissolved in the dishwater of sentiment. *Deiri*, my Irish teacher said: from *Dei*, "tears" meaning exile—one who has known tears. She told how a queen had reclaimed the city from marsh by swallowing all the waters, and if anyone leapt into the River Lee and milked her nipples, all the waters of the world would stream out. The tale spiked the suicide rate, she teased, with so many lovers leaping off Patrick's Bridge. But fishing in the sink's gristled mire for a fork, I knew that a queen's breasts wouldn't ooze for me. Nor for McCann, lurching in subway din. Finally he must have known that no muse or captain had sent him after all. And it's no myth he came from: there are no breasts under the North's crust, only coal. Maybe Finbar, scion of Spanish swimmers, could steal a lick. But not Francis McCann, and not me.

Last summer, twenty years after my first trip to Ireland, I sat in the lobby of a posh Cork hotel so placeless they served martinis. By this time, there was little that Captain America and his minions hadn't zapped to homogeneity. No longer could I climb to Gurranabraher and stand among sheep. Cork was choked with suburbs and roundabouts, malls and billboards. Apartment complexes sprouted satellite dishes; bistros served up exotic cuisine. Even the plumbing was impeccable. I was back in Ireland for an international conference, a professor myself now, though not on a par with the crow-robes who'd quarreled with Emmett and O'Connell. And there, two tables down, was Finbar himself, looking just like his book-jacket photo.

I went over and tapped his shoulder. "Hello, you're Finbar, aren't you?"

He half-turned, used to this—able to size up the Yank by voice, one of the multitude.

"Finbar," I said. "Don't you know me?" tendering dual profiles.

"No, should I?" he answered, all the Cork distilled out of his voice.

When I told him how we'd met, his black eyebrows arched, remapping the lines of his face, and I glimpsed for an instant the boyo of pizza fame. In his swamp-thick brogue, put on now for effect, he regaled our colleagues around the sectional lounge couch, while waiters, like shadows filleted from our pasts, glided by.

Sitting tonight before this blue screen in Ohio, the map of Ireland winking, Mary snoring, Finbar spoke to me again, his arched eyebrows and forsaken Cork brogue almost present in the e-mail signals blipped across the ocean.

"It was great if slightly eerie to meet you again so unexpectedly," he wrote. "It's a terrible shock sometimes to find out how much memory is locked in sealed boxes."

Sealed up, sealed away—all the waters of the world. Now the dissonant echoes start to blend:

"You're doing fook all back here."

"Look at the fire, oh the fire looks good."

"Nostrand Avenue, next."

It's the blurring of designs that stamps rage down into the sultry mud. Tonight I feel the sinks, mines, river, bars, and subways blending and spreading like a muddy bruise. No wonder we sway—Mary and I—with all the journeys heaving underfoot: my parents ogling jets, Pet ducking under a subway stile, Francis McCann and I crossing each other's paths over the ocean.

Imagine it, Goddess: McCann holding his pillar of coins, me pursing my hands over my cherubic balls. Perhaps in the eye of the Spanish olive brining the duty-free Cork Dry Gin martini we did meet. Perhaps that moment of crossing, this of swallowing, capsized design. Maybe that's all there is to you: grandfather and grandson passing through each other, each causing the other to be, joined in the spark I saw in Mary's eyes. For all the Dramamine, on the day of my first sea-crossing my stomach sank toward the Atlantic—maybe toward the very wave that crested in McCann's stomach seventy years ago. Booze and dance—your most constant surrogates—tonight at least, have effaced time. I cradle my head between my knees and see ocean. McCann's eyes roll due north from the steerage berth, where he huddles with Sarah and four girls, peering at the unfamiliar sky, catching in the clouds a glimpse of your singing, dissolving face.

7.

FRANCIS & THE SUITORS

If design govern in a thing so small.
—ROBERT FROST

No wonder Mary seems likely to bury us all, though spider-shriveled, shuttled from Ulster to Brooklyn to Flushing, back to Brooklyn and now to Ohio. After all, it was for her sake that McCann minted his new American design. This was no blind hoarding of coins, no Goddess-quest. Hurtling through the subways beneath Brooklyn, McCann conceived a plan more complex than the IRT, one meant to hoist his daughters aboveground implacably as engines winched the leviathan up to the El.

For the wee girls, Betty, Kay, and Pet, he had years to prepare; they could be left to Sarah. All she had to do, he believed, was swat them off to school each morning and at night deliver sermons against the Flatbush hooligans. From his bar stool at Duffy's speakeasy, McCann monitored the changes: hair teased into flips, accents flattening. But for Mary he needed to do something now. She was already twenty-two when they crossed the ocean, too old to remake her in the image of the country they were stranded in. How provide for her?

Trapped in his male maze, McCann may not have understood his American girls, but he knew what it took to leaven his eldest daughter's fortunes. But how to choose a husband in this strange place with its neon signs and thick steaks and barbarous talk? So McCann devised a test for Mary's beaus. How many there were I don't know. I have only one photo of Mary from that time: a pallid figure in striped frock, with no hint of the elemental permanence the almost eighty years since have carved into her face. But one candidate at least, Dick Martin, was summoned on a Saturday night late in 1922 to Duffy's speakeasy, where Francis McCann repaired to read American newspapers and take refuge from the noisy yeasting of his offspring. He consumed straight black tea, perched on his high stool, knees cocked, brogues hooked in the brass foot rail, awaiting the appearance of a son.

Duffy's is legal now, though little else has changed—the gouged mahogany, the laurelled mirror. One June evening after a high school baseball game under the eerie lights of Randall's Island, my father took me there. I was seventeen, bloused in my Fordham Prep baseball regalia—kangaroo spikes and all—fresh from repeating over and over with my lanky body the motion that generated a flash of stitched horsehide through the midgey tunnel of night. And after pitching a three-hitter through six innings and somehow coming to myself and getting knocked out in the seventh, I searched the bleachers for my father's face, and gave him a look that showed I was finally finished being the exquisite animal he'd trained. And for that look, better than winning, I was apotheosized over the Triboro for my initiation into manhood.

Duffy's is *Dubh*, meaning Dark, redolent of doomed love—Dark Rosaleen, Dark Island. It was a ramshackle tomb, the notched bar stained with half-moons, sheela-na-gigs leering from the crannies. And there was Duffy, not the original but his son, a freckle-faced curate with a head so big that if you capped it, you'd have a police force. He nodded at my father as his father must have nodded at McCann. Wordless, he pulled the throttle on two pint glasses, set them to burble on the bar, while I spun on my stool to survey the dank-suited Micks hunched over brackish jars, their faces as carbuncled as the ancient map of Ireland on the wall. When I swiveled back, Duffy had the two porters in his mitts, and he tipped the shaft forward with his pinky, gently as a lit candle, brimming the first then the second pint glass to the rim, the cream tickling the air. He pucked them down in front of us. My first pint. I peered into the thumbprinted cream glaze and raised the glass to my mouth, tasting a bitterness I'd never known—nothing like the noggin of rage I'd spat on the baseline as I stamped off the Randall's Island diamond. Catching my reflection in the mirror, my father laughed.

"Need a straw there, Moose?" he asked.

"This is cool," I said, eyeing the parade of exotic vessels— Campari, Pernod, Jack Daniel's, Paddy's, Tanqueray, Southern Comfort. My father wiped his mouth and winked at Duffy, who planted his elbows on the mahogany, studying my outfit.

Leaning in, my father said, "Here's a pitch you rookies might not have seen before." Drawing his wallet from his trouser pocket, he plucked out a twenty and smoothed the dog-ears on the bar. Then he began the story of McCann's test for future sons-in-law.

Dick Martin, taciturn Presbyterian in gorse tweed, fingernails black with the tulipy soil of the Long Island estate where he worked as gardener, passed under the rooftree of Duffy's Tavern. He'd never met McCann. Whenever he drove his clapped-out Ford back to Brooklyn to see Mary, it was Sarah who greeted him, petted him, offering tea and soda bread (with a glance toward the jug in the cupboard) while Mary primped. Now Dick Martin was summoned, alone, to Duffy's, site of the dread inter- view. Not hard to spot the judge: a man spare as himself, cheeks hollowed to spoons, still wearing his transport regulars, sipping tea, spectacles scanning lurid print. Martin buttoned his jacket, gave Duffy the farmer's nod, and approached.

"Mr. McCann, sir," offering a blunt right hand.

"Ah, boy, you're here. What will you have," signaling Duffy.

This was the opening gambit.

"Tea, like yourself, sir, but with a sup o' milk," and the outer portal opened. McCann signaled to Duffy Pére, who turned back to the kitchen, rolling his eyes at these two abstemious north- men. McCann shifted on his stool.

"And what is it exactly you do, Mr. Martin? How does a lad strike a path in New York today?" asked McCann, wasting no time.

"The work is steady. I'm gardener at Garrett's, beyond in Hempstead," said Martin warily, knowing McCann had been briefed about Martin's post, which Mary had described in florid detail, trying to pass over her beau's religion.

But churches meant nothing to McCann, indifferent as he was to the rage that had torn Ulster apart above his head. This second question, posed as Duffy placed a steaming teapot on the bar, was meant to keep his prey talking, to puppet his eyes level as McCann flourished his wallet from his hip, letting slip as if unnoticed a twenty-dollar bill, as my father showed me, tweezing his twenty from the bar with a flip of ring finger and pinky, letting it float to the floor. As McCann pretended to listen to Martin describe Babylon, he fixed his eyes on Martin's eyes, as my father's gray eyes riveted mine. McCann, at least, saw what he needed. A flicker of distaste crossed Martin's face: a man unaccustomed to planting dollars in sawdust. By the time the young gardener had reached down to retrieve the twenty and return it to my grandfather, saying, with a tight smile, "I think you dropped this Scotsman, sir, and he might come in handy," he was already McCann's son.

Six months after his visit to Duffy's, Martin carried off his bride from St. Teresa's Church with all the panoply his Ford's horn could muster, bound for the mythical gardens of Long Island, leaving McCann well pleased. At least he knew his daughter's name would never figure in the strange accounts he studied in the news.

Two years later, Mary was a widow with an infant child. I don't know what his son-in-law's death meant to McCann, aside from the untimely return of his eldest daughter and her unhappy child. But a man of McCann's mettle wasn't easily turned from a plan once made. When the time came to shrive Betty's suitor, McCann waited at Duffy's prepared for the worst. She was the bane of her mother's life, a firebrand determined since puberty to kick the dust of McCann's cold-water flat from her heels. What kind of yahoo would Betty offer up?

She was the prettiest, they all said, repeating it like doctrine, but by the time I knew Aunt Betty, whatever looks she'd boasted were pasted over with an unwrinkled purpose. Her face was dented at the temples as if squeezed by calipers; her hair, once "auburn," I was told—not "red"—was bleached numb, the print-marks of rollers sprayed in permanently. Though she had a son and daughter and a husband, her row house across the street from ours was kept as taut as a museum, no toy or newspaper or glass or cigarette butt visible; beds hospital-tucked, kitchen furious with chrome—immaculate as the moon.

My two cousins called their mother "ma'am," preceded only by "yes." As far as I could tell, Uncle Tom was confined to the garage. On grim occasions, I was yanked across to 53-17 to visit, and the children were paroled and the garage door left ajar for Tom to tiptoe up the stoop, his breath spicing the air. Our thighs stuck to plastic-wrapped chairs and couch. Pet's eyes hunted for an ashtray. My brother and I fidgeted until Aunt Betty froze us, warning of two creatures, Snarlygob and Harrion, who crouched behind the gilded lattice in her end tables, ready to leap out and claw the eyes off brats who scuffed, picked, smudged. They prowled my dreams for years.

So one Saturday in mid-Depression, when Tom Halloran barged through Duffy's tavern door, McCann barely glanced up from the newspaper. He made no remark when Halloran, a whisky at his elbow, chatting away about his plans to start an ice-cream shop in Elmhurst, placed a hobnailed toe on McCann's dropped bill.

At home that night, McCann made a last stand. "Sundaes, the man says. Peppermint, is it? I'd sooner invest in the still he takes drink from. Now there's a good business."

No use. Betty was determined to marry with or without her father's investment or consent, and McCann's design melted before her countenance.

If I didn't know Aunt Betty, I could hardly have imagined the Tom Halloran who strolled out of Duffy's that night in 1937 up twenty bucks and one fiancée: brawler, gambler, and drunk. On our tense visits, all he brought up from the garage was a wink and racy breath. But I see now that Snarlygob roamed inside him as Harrion possessed his wife, and even gold lattice could not cage their demons.

Kay was the flighty one, with a gin-mill laugh and a bee's attention span. Even in her seventies she wore cubes of costume jewelry and painted the air with scarlet fingernails. What did a world war mean to her? No need to wait for the soldiers to return. She flitted through the dance halls and settled on Terry Dolan, 4-F. Summoned to Duffy's, Dolan tooled up in a spiffy Buick, left Kay double-parked, and sashayed into the bar in gray sharkskin, the whole life of America whizzing by so fast that there wasn't time to fully form his face.

"Hey, Mr. McCann, nice to meetcha."

McCann nodded—a Coney Island Pharaoh.

"What will you have, boy?"

"A beer, thanks," touching McCann's sleeve.

By now McCann was going through the motions, stripping gears over the wreckage of his plans: his first son-in-law's death, his daughter's return to Brooklyn with a granddaughter, and the fecklessness of his second son-in-law (for all her cooing on the foyer phone, Sarah couldn't hide the fact that the dropped twenty wasn't the last licked off him by the ice-cream king). Still, McCann conducted the timeworn test, dropping the double-sawback on question two. But Dolan's gaze just kept sailing. Disgusted, McCann finally had to bend down and reel in the lure himself.

"Hey, whaddaya know?" said Dolan when McCann picked the bill off the floor. "Anybody around here lose a twenty?"

It wasn't long before Dolan proved the army right, haunting the clinics and hospitals—"If it isn't an ass it's an elbow," Kay would laugh, rolling her eyes under tarantula lashes. And Dolan passed on his rickety genes, his unmade batter face, to his son. Still, whatever wobbly dance world Kay and Terry Dolan boogied in, they never wanted another. They barricaded themselves in their flat on Sterling Place for forty years.

Once, a few years ago, my mother came home from Bishop Boardman and told us she drove right past them downtown—Kay and Terry—strolling arm in arm, laughing, oblivious to their borough's transformation. She didn't even honk. Who'd notice?

By the time the war ended and Phil Brady had returned from France to claim the bride he'd wooed with daily letters for three years, McCann had given up. He'd seen his first son-in-law die, the second broke and jobless, and the third stuck in a sickroom. Still, Pet coaxed him out, and he soldiered down Prospect Avenue to Duffy's, ordered his tea, and unfolded his newspaper, summoning the last suitor as Phil Brady summoned me, flashing me the twenty-dollar bill as once it had been shown to him.

Phil Brady in 1945 was a slab of brawn, bucktoothed, light-footed. He could wiggle his ears, make wall-shadow rabbits, and pass a blindfold test of seven brands of scotch. Returned from the war, where he'd rollicked through Europe liberating brandy cellars, he was poised to start a new job on the Force and undaunted by the future that would carry him through marriage, career, children, heart attacks, strokes, and cancer.

That evening, Phil Brady couldn't have known his future, but he'd been warned of McCann's flimflam and did him one better. When the twenty slipped, an afterthought, from the old man's hand, Phil Brady bent slowly, twitched his sleeve, and reappeared with a grin, holding, as he showed me at Duffy's the June night he drove me across the Triboro into manhood, a crisp new fifty-dollar bill.

I hear his punch line now, in Ohio, as Duffy's son and I heard it at Duffy's—where McCann heard it in wonder, in 1945, finally arriving in the America of his dreams.

"You dropped this, father," my father said, "and I think you might be needing it."

They don't need any hocus-pocus now. But I do.

8.

FATHER'S MILK

My father has gone wild into his grave.
—King Henry IV Part II

Fishing through news clippings, cards, letters, and glue-encrusted photos filed in an old footlocker, I try to imagine my father in the first flush of manhood, returning from war to join the Police Force, poised for the Herculean labor of straightening things out. There were car-theft rings to crack, milk-robbers to nab. Someone had to foil the poolroom scam, grab the ether out of the lunatic's mitt. I won't need a Goddess to tell this story. The legacy of my father's career has been preserved.

Murry Samuels, 48-year-old Forest Hills milk dealer who accused his wife of consorting with a burglar, goes to Ridgewood Felony Court today charged with stealing milk from other dealers to supply his own customers. Samuels lives at 67-71 Yellowstone Boulevard and operates Fairchild Farms, a two-milkman company. He was arrested yesterday by Detective Phil Brady of the Jamaica Estates

North Squad, who said Samuels picked up several cases of milk
from store doors where it had been delivered by other dealers, and
also helped himself to the bagels left by a baker. Brady dogged
Samuels to a store in Flatbush and collared him there. The milk
was worth $150, Brady said.

Before I could safely sit at my desk, listening to the refrigerator
throb, watching buds shiver on the rain-slicked tree, my father
had to clear the way by confronting David Fleigenheimer, gone
berserk, attacking wife and seven-year-old daughter with an
ice pick, a penknife, and a nail file. He had to charge him with
forcing ether down his wife's throat, setting fire to the bed
where she lay bleeding, cracking a .22-caliber rifle on the child's
head, smashing the wood stock.

Were it not for the olive footlocker I have inherited, stuffed
with old solutions, would I find bodies sprawled across my
threshold, lying in blood, wrists slashed? Would I piece together
clues, revealing this story to an unnamed source? I could interro-
gate the crooks whose schemes are recorded here: the ex-con who
crashed his jalopy into a bar, then slammed down three shots to
beat the drunk driving rap, or the bank robbery suspect who
unbuttoned his shirt to show his lawyer his bruised kidneys, or
my Aunt, who hums, "the time, the time it is do you remember
that." But no one who lived in Detective Brady's chaos will
snitch; every ghost's tight-lipped.

This was the task my father undertook, along with so many
other GIs returning from Europe: to straighten, to solve, to
crack, to dog. Soon after he turned in his Military Police sergeant
stripes, his silky voice and typing skills landed him a post as
secretary to Police Commissioner O'Brien. Here's his newspaper
photo, March 20, 1949: a young buck in a suave brown suit
handing his boss a sheaf of papers. And here's a glossy of the
1951 St. Patrick's Day parade, rows of brass-buttoned tunics and
white gloves saluting, eyes left toward the platform from which
Cardinal Spellman confers a blessing. You can just make out Phil
Brady, fourth row center. After only three years in uniform, he
earned his detective's shield, and his initiative in the milk caper
got him promoted to second grade. By 1961, he was in homicide,
first-grade detective, top of the line. In 1965, though, the news

clippings and commendations end abruptly. And for 1966, there's only one souvenir, a cream card embossed with a badge featuring two figures leaning on a coat of arms, an eagle rampant, Shield 566, City of New York Police Detective. It's an invitation to my father's retirement party, which I remember only because it was on that occasion that I wore, at the age of ten, my first real tie.

I stare at the card and read in it another mystery: a man not much older than I am now, with two children, gives up a career on the Police Force to run security for the Board of Education? Something unrecorded in this box thwarted my father in his mission to remake the world. Instead, from 1966 on, he bent all his powers on remaking me.

It was as if he had designed my body, could marshal it. Weeknights from April to October, after the bombast of dinner had died down and my mother had climbed the stairs to call Aunt Mary, my father and I scraped back our opposite chairs and skipped down to the basement, where I yanked open the creaky tin cabinet, pulled down the Joe Torre catcher's mitt and the pitcher's glove coning a scuffed ball, and followed his shoulders through the screen door. The sixty feet six inches was paced off from the manhole cover and marked with a needle of spit. Between these poles, as dusk ignited the streetlights, we tested the dynamics of myth. Each nuance was choreographed: toe pointed to crotch of the fire hydrant, thigh flexed, impossibly, a moment before the pivot torqued the ten-, the twelve-, the sixteen-year-old body that was his mind into a slash forward, gyring toward the future.

Though the ball smacked into the pocket, somehow it never quite resolved. Some kink in the delivery imparted a cosmic english, just as the world my father set out to fix eluded him in the nineteen-sixties, corkscrewing like a Heisenberg spitball from Sinatra to the Stones, parishes to communes, the Duke to the Dalai Lama, Normandy to My Lai.

Still my father yearned to sail, in my body, beyond the torrent of change he'd sworn to shield me from, to transcend the two-bit cases he'd cracked on the Force and continued to file at Borough Hall: the hoods stuffing a hippie into a garbage can; the gym teacher scoring pot from the janitor. Even the diocesan schools seemed inadequate, pedestrian, drained of Latin and grandeur by Vatican II.

This is the only alibi I can concoct for him, the only explanation I have for the four years when I was rousted out of bed every weekday morning before dawn, starting at puberty, to knot a maroon tie, belt Korvette slacks, and sojourn to the Bronx, to Fordham Prep—the only high school in the city with a university on its campus. That's how the headmaster, Father Eugene J. O'Brien, with a sumptuous voice and a handshake smoother than single malt, described it to the sycophants gathered in the university banquet room for freshman orientation. It was the softest, most delicate of sales, but dazzling enough to fleece my father of sense and tuition and to make me forget the complete absence of girls and the daily grind of three bus routes. There was the Q76 from Francis Lewis to College Point to the Q44 across the Whitestone Bridge, whose view of bay and skyline afforded the day's only tranquil moment, and finally the BX20, which sucked up a gaggle of preppies from the trash heaps of West Farms Square, delivering us to Rose Hill, the jewel in the belly of the South Bronx. There, in my father's mind, I'd be dipped to the gills in classics and casuistry. But even the Jesuits had been dizzied in the whirlwind. Despite Father O'Brien's high-hatted welcome, they were no longer the Jansenists Simon Dedalus revered.

In 1970, the Berrigan brothers preached revolution from a priest hole. The Ramskeller was rank with pot smoke. The SDS marked the second anniversary of the Tet Offensive by torching the campus center. In Lit class, it was Ginsberg and Mailer; in Religion, folk mass and JC Superstar. And after the spine-jolting bus ride home, there was the dinner table. The clash of plates, the stirring of stews and soups, wafted from far away like thunder or artillery, while my father and I fed on words, stripped of meaning. There were the newscasts, the body counts, the shavings of misapprehended thought, the slatherings of nostalgia for baseball players and Irish mayors; the nonsense spiraling into an ideal, impossible, shared world.

It could begin anywhere. A question about English homework could spark conjectures on the etymology of "justice" which veered to Marxist praxis, which somehow detoured into marijuana and brain damage. By the time the casserole was scooped, we'd have escalated to Hammurabi and the Holy Ghost. Night after night the battle raged without a voice raised or a fact checked, until Brian's slouch left him at eye-level with his melting ice cream. Finally Pet would throw up her hands, signaling an end with her stock line, "A plague on both your houses."

Right to the end we manned opposite illusions, my father and I, without even a ball to thread the distance. Even after he lost speech and continence, his mammoth body shrunk, still we contested. As he slumped behind his TV tray, his bandaged toe oozing blood, I'd shave him when I visited, stroking his rubbery throat.

"Yes, Dad, I read that," I'd say. "Buckley has a point, but . . . ." Like him, I remained entrenched, unwilling to surrender.

Bathed in cathode rays, we languished in the efficiency at Mirror Lake, oblivious to weather, to sickness, to the pressure of the past that tightened around our heads like metal bands. I'd scrape the razor over his mealy jowls as he worked the TV remote control, flipping through kaleidoscopic images: face, horse, tree, explosion, ocean, ball field, tower, horrible insect. What he was ever looking for, I don't know.

Once I heard a name I couldn't believe I'd heard, a name promising to augur truce. I snatched the remote from his yellow fingers and turned back, and there she was: Ellen Barkin, that Goddess of Queens, on the Letterman show, sitting cross-legged, voluptuous. Suddenly, the past—the real one, the one we could never talk about—exploded. I lifted the razor from my father's cheek. I could almost hear the sizzle of the shaving soap as she spoke it again—"Alice Crimmins."

"Did you hear that, Dad?" I blurted, squeezing his shoulder. "This movie star knew Alice."

The TV, as if it had been tuned to an alien channel only my father and I could receive, told the story: in 1965, this Queens divorcee had been tried and convicted for the murder of her two children. And Ellen Barkin, sultry star of many a cop flick, had grown up right next door to what turned out to be my father's famous case. After all the milk-robbers, wife-beaters, racketeers and swindlers, he'd been assigned a double homicide, and years later a book was published, *The Alice Crimmins Case*, which described my mother as "a perky redhead" and made my father sound like a priestly Jack Webb.

"Do you remember, Dad? Do you remember the Alice Crimmins case?"

His hand levitated, waving me off.

"You didn't think she did it, remember? She visited us, at 53-28, when you were on the case."

"Ah, Alice . . . Crimmins," he stuttered and raised a hand as if to keep her presence off.

"Yes, you defended her. All the other cops thought she was guilty. I read the book."

But his hand wavered toward the box, and I surrendered the remote, shook my head, and retreated to the tiny kitchen, rummaging in the fridge.

"Today is the fiftieth anniversary of Normandy," I heard in newscast baritone which blared louder as my father's finger poked the volume.

"Nor, Nor-man-dy," he said, shaking his head. I came back and stood behind the recliner, a beer in hand.

"Yes, Dad, June 6—fifty years ago today. You were there, too. Do you remember?"

"No, no, winter. February. In the winter."

His hand jerked as if plucked on puppet strings.

"February? Dad, it was June. June 6th. Fifty years."

"Feb, February," he insisted.

I gazed sullenly at his lathered face. How many times had we quibbled trivia? So I just let go. Fine, it was deep in February. The whitecaps, the dark sea hissing on the French shore, snow banking German pillboxes. Is this what he had longed for? The goal of all his straightening? Not Brooklyn or the Bronx, not Ireland or Utopia. Just death, solitary, silent. And he could wait no longer, my father. The enemy was beyond; he faced them now. Nothing to defend. June too far off.

After he died, sunk under four strokes and liver cancer, I told Pet about our last skirmish, about Normandy. But he hadn't been talking about the war at all, she explained. He'd been talking about a ship in New York harbor called *The Normandy* that had been torched by arsonists in February of 1946. My father had worked this case too, one of the thousands.

About Alice, I said nothing. Her story I must tell myself, because it is my story too.

53

9.

WIRETAP

I am walking backward into the future like a Greek.
—MICHAEL LONGLEY

WHEN I was growing up, the denizens of Queens walked like Dante's sodomites: heads and feet cranked arsewards. Everyone went both ways, baleful gazes aiming westward toward Manhattan's hordes, nipples stiffened toward the prefab paradise of Long Island.

The fear and desire that unscrewed my head and cranked it around was Father. My own first, but not just him: there was Monsignor Barry, the martinet who drilled altar boys in liturgical Latin; and later, Jack Sullivan, crew-cut maniac coach of Fordham Prep, who'd skip full-jacketed into the shower for hugs. I puppied after teachers, jocks, movie stars, anything with a codpiece.

It is possible to travel a long way so contorted. Last year, my breastbone pointed toward the seacoast of West Cork and my head screwed backward toward the cottage where the latest incarnation of my father, a famous poet, one of the Cork crow-robes, ate his lunch.

In 1975, it had taken three day's nerve to mount the stairs to his office. Taking a breath, I'd knocked and, hearing a muffled grunt, turned the knob and entered the dim, musty sanctum crammed with books. Pictures hung askew—an inked Joyce, a chieftain's death mask. On the bare floorboards sat a desk spavined with tomes, and behind, silhouetted in twilight, roosted the poet, his Norman head with its crest of white hair floating above the turtleneck of a fisherman's knit sweater. His eyes were recessed deep under his brow, and tiny blue deltas marked his ruddy cheeks.

Opening a fist whose swan ring spread over two knuckles, he seated me, and after a few sweating clock-ticks I blurted that he and I came from the same neighborhood, then gushed a line of one of his poems I'd learned rocking at the cabinet hi-fi. The poet canted his aquiline nose and, sidestepping my faux pas, asked how well I knew Brooklyn, where he'd spent childhood years before returning to Ireland.

"My parents," I confessed.

He swiveled toward the tiny window, and sighing, said it was past time. I jumped to my feet, pivoted to the door, but he continued, "Past time for a pint, don't you think?"

"Yes, if you mean, I mean, that's great," I stammered.

He led me down the stairs and out into the wind of Western Road, and we matched strides past the Lee eddy with its green phone booth, past Fr. Matthew's statue and the Patrick Street Cinema featuring *Jaws*, down the alley of Oliver Plunkett Street, and into the musky warmth of the Long Valley, a tiled barroom with Tiffany lamps and trays of crustless sandwiches and radishes and celery stalks and slabs of soda bread. The poet wended through the late-afternoon crowd and seated himself at an oval stone-heavy table, beckoning the two Murphy's pints the barman had brought unbidden. With a pencil tweezed from his breast pocket, he nibbed dashes and question marks in the margins of the poem I'd pressed on him, all the while humming to the barman's flow of chatter about Hitler's private life. And so the night slid by—a blur of pints and faces—students, fans, dossers, and prognosticators dropping by to spar with the poet and check out the Yank.

"It's an arid place for the spirit, the States is," said one curly-haired youth with granny glasses and a red-and-white tasseled scarf, stinging me into a paean to Robert Bly, the Great Mother Goddess conference, yoga retreats, astrology, and free love.

Twitching an eyebrow, the poet said, "I wonder if Bly isn't just a mad Protestant farmer."

He knew everyone on both sides—Berryman and Lowell and Williams and Roethke and Kavanagh and Gogarty and Clarke and Beckett. He'd shared poteen with Behan and tea with Mrs. Yeats and fly-fished with Ted Hughes and crossed the Bay Bridge on the back of Gary Snyder's motorcycle, and he gossiped as if they were a pack of quarrelsome neighbors. It was the first of many magical evenings, ending with weak-kneed ambles through the sleeping city to Tivoli in mist that always seemed wetter than American rain.

Over the years, I tracked his zigzagging from Albany to Cork to San Francisco to Pittsburgh, and when I'd spot him I'd elbow through the small throng of hangers-on, unfolding my newest aspirations, which, if I got him alone, he would chevron with arabesques, humming, slinging koans.

"Who are your contemporaries?" he asked once, making me think of my struggling school friends, all of us angling for a passport to Parnassus. And I remember the searching look he gave me when he said, "Every poet has a secret wound."

After a gala reading at the 92nd Street Y in New York, he bunked the night at 53-28, and that evening Phil Brady chauffeured us on one of his city tours, cruising through Queens pointing out the locations of famous benders, mob deals, and shoot-outs. After one spine-tingling swerve around a traffic snarl, we ended up at Peter Luger's steak house in Brooklyn, with its charred rafters and creamed spinach and waiters looking like refugees from the Luftwaffe. My heart still pounding from the near-accident, I darted glances from father to father as they traded tales of politicos, crooks, and gunmen as exotic as Gods and Fighting Men. I realized that the poet wouldn't have to ask about my wound.

That's how I came last year to be guest, cook, and driving instructor at the cottage where he spent months each year with Mia, a black-haired pixie from Sarah Lawrence, younger than I was. I picked my way over the sheep-dipped gorse into the kitchen, where the pair bent over the deal table, spooning bowls of my stew.

"Not bad," the poet lied.

I shrugged, tossed a wreath of keys onto the table, and said, "Let's take a spin."

We crossed the path to the antique Ibuzu I'd bought from the local garage, and I folded my legs into the right side, forgetting that everything here is backward. My pupils watched me slide into the death seat then climbed in after, and as the poet worried the stick shift, I palmed his hand, saying, "It's easy, remember? Down first, then over. And gentle with the clutch." I thought of quoting his lines, "changing gears with/ the same gesture as/ eased your snowbound/ heart and flesh," but, remembering my gaffe on the day we first met, I bit my tongue.

"Reverse, you bastard," the poet said, and the buggy spasmed backward, scattering sheep.

Over Mount Gabriel we threaded unshouldered paths to Schull, a small crescent inlet of the sea, where we lurched to a stop and disembarked, light-headed, for an afternoon pint. Soon we were safely squatting on three-legged stools by a turf fire.

"To luck," I lifted my glass, "we'll need it to cross back over that mountain."

"We barely outran our shadow," the poet scoffed. "New York's where the real slaughter goes on," he turned to his girl-friend and described how my father, one finger on the wheel, had driven us through the back streets of Brooklyn, pointing out scenes of obscure calumny. The tour and our lives almost ended when my father drifted in mid-sentence through a stop sign into boulevard traffic.

"If that's how you learned to drive," Mia said, "what kind of murderers will you make of us?"

The barman, a giant with a reckless black beard, brought us our pints and disappeared into the lounge. Leaning in conspiratorially, the poet whispered, "This is Bailey's local, you know." I took in the small stone room, pewter mugs on the mantle, a lacquered oar and harpoon displayed on the wall.

"Is that why it's empty?" I asked.

These days the mention of Ian Bailey stirred murmurs even in empty rooms. He was one of the army of "blow-ins" who swarmed into West Cork seeking a haven, wayfarers of all stripes, from Tony Blair and Jeremy Irons, whose summer homes were nestled under the shadow of Mount Gabriel, all the way down to the Austrian palm-reader who ran a tea shop in Bally-dehob and the paparazzi who retired from chasing Princess Di to do photo shoots of "Writers on Bicycles." The local grocery store was run by Oregon hippies; yoga seminars were advertised on pub doors.

An aspiring poet and journalist, Bailey had come from Liverpool to West Cork, took up the bodhrán, jazzed his name to Eoin O'Baille, hired out as the poet's gardener, and, like so many of us, slipped verses under his pencil. But all Bailey's aspirations had darkened one morning six months before, when the body of Sophie Toscan du Plantier, a beautiful thirty-nine-year-old French woman, wife of a French film producer, was discovered lying a hundred feet from her holiday home in Toormoor, near Schull. It was Bailey, working as a stringer for the Cork *Examiner*, who'd broken the story, and his intimate knowledge of the crime scene raised questions about the nature of his source. The victim's skull had been smashed with a blunt instrument—a club or hammer, he'd reported. There'd been no sign of robbery or sexual assault, and the Gardai wondered if the assailant was known by the victim; who else but a neighbor or acquaintance would be let in so late at night? Rumors swirled that an opened bottle of wine and two washed glasses had been found on the kitchen table. There were whispers that Bailey had confessed, saying, "I went too far." The only other suspect was a German businessman who committed suicide, leaving a note that vaguely implicated him in "something bad." But nothing could be proved, and though the Gardai had arrested Bailey twice, both times they'd released him, to the chagrin of the French government, which saw the botched investigation as an international affront.

Anywhere else this might have been stale news, but here, just a few miles from the spot where Michael Collins had been ambushed, politics had always been the main motive for killing. The poet's eyes glinted with intrigue. Was it a failed love affair? Attempted rape?

"It could have been anyone," he said. "West Cork's swarming with sex mechanics."

"Listen," I said, "why don't I go see Bailey. I have my father's badge. I'll tell him I'm a New York cop brought here to consult. He wants to be a journalist. Here's his chance."

"You gobshite," the poet snorted. "Don't you know everyone already knows who you are. You can't wipe your arse around here without the world and his brother holding his nose."

And so, as the bar darkened, the talk having turned to murder, I slipped a poem out of my jacket pocket and asked the poet if he wouldn't take a look.

"It's about my father," I said. "It's a few years old. About the Crimmins case. I've been reworking it."

"The poem or the murder?" he asked, as he patted his vest for a pencil. "You haven't heard about this, I think, my dear. Tell Mia about Alice."

The poet took a sturdy pull on his pint and scraped his stool to the fire as I told my fellow New Yorker about my father's case.

One August evening, midway between World War Two and now, my brother and I were called in from the amniotic air of 194th Street and scrubbed and swatted upstairs. The vacuum roared; the liquor cabinet drawbridged to reveal emerald and gold bottles; polished ashtrays garnished the end tables. Tonight, coming for cocktails: Alice Crimmins, whose picture was blazoned on the front page of the *Daily News*, looking like Jackie Kennedy with scarf and sunglasses.

Alice lived the life that was not admitted to exist in Queens. She had affairs and drank bourbon in low-life bars. She divorced, remarried the same man, divorced him again. She faced straight ahead, didn't swerve around priest or cop. Maybe that's why she wore sunglasses at night. When her children went missing on the night of June 23, it didn't take the detectives long to point fingers. Though there were no witnesses and no physical evidence, though the first detective on the scene botched the crime-scene photos, though Alice had no conceivable motive to murder her children, the investigation torqued down on her. The evidence: the men, the booze, the sunglasses.

"If she was my wife, I'd kill her," one dick growled. But they only had to break her, and they set about grilling her at the precinct, buttonholing her boyfriends, harassing the offices where she did temp work under an assumed name. Her estranged husband they dismissed as a fool and cuckold without brains or guts enough to govern his wife, much less kill his children.

On the day, two weeks after the disappearance, when they found the missing girl under a hedge near the old World's Fair site, they brought Alice to identify the decaying corpse without warning her about what she was about to see. She fainted on the spot—more proof of guilt—the theatrical ploy, when she'd shown no grief till then. During the months that followed, she continued to drink and dance and lure men back to her Kew Gardens apartment: a Mafioso, a Long Island real estate shark, even a cop. Guilty, guilty, guilty. But how prove it?

So they brought in Phil Brady: plaid-lapelled, purse-lipped, with a priest's bearing, peacock pheromones and a voice that fluttered the hearts of waitresses. Though he was a CYO coach, Holy Name bigwig, and church usher, head cranked back to the Catholic fantasy of Queens, nose listing to port, there was, inside his florid body, an emerald that changed hue, emanating from each facet a different mood.

Because of his MP technical experience, eavesdropping from Normandy to Bohemia, he was called into the Alice Crimmins case not to investigate but to listen, assigned to wiretap Alice's apartment, her car, the booth in her local tavern. He sat in a dark van listening to her lovemaking, her weeping, her cursing. This was his gift, a gift I never knew he had: to listen, to absorb the confessions of others and remain himself. Though the Alice Crimmins case spun the heads of the NYPD, there was a place inside Phil Brady that nobody was going to touch.

That August night when Alice rang the doorbell, I sneaked out of bed and crawled to the top of the stairs to glimpse between the banister rails the famed murderess in a flame cocktail dress, highball in one hand, cigarette in the other, laughing and talking, sitting cross-legged on the couch. My father was hunched forward, my mother perched in her orange Queen Anne chair, swinging her crossed leg in time to the Mitch Miller LP playing on the hi-fi, and suddenly, I felt the weather change. Alice shrank into herself, her beehive bobbing with cramped sobs. My mother's leg froze; my father rose from his recliner and glided like a bearish cloud to the couch. Whispering, he draped his huge arm over her shoulder. I'd never seen him hold my mother the way he held Alice that night, and she sobbing and sobbing.

What I didn't learn until years later, when I read *The Alice Crimmins Case*, is that our basement had been as carefully prepared for Alice's visit as the rest of the house. There, amid the flotsam of unmatched socks and old trophies, three detectives hunkered over a massive tape recorder. What could they have made of what they heard—a scratchy voice whispering, "There, there?" A woman's sobs? Maybe the hidden mikes were sensitive enough to catch the pounding of a child's heart.

Telling the story in a quiet pub in the penumbra of another murder, I conjured Alice Crimmins, Goddess, mounting the stairs quietly to my childhood.

"How did it end?" Mia asked.

"She was convicted, finally, after two trials. Served eight years. I heard that she moved to Florida when she got out. She'd be in her eighties now, if she's alive."

"Did you write this before your father died?" the poet asked, having turned back to us now, his glass empty.

"Yes."

"Did you show him?"

"All he said was, 'you got some facts wrong.' Nothing about the poem—about him and me and how I couldn't ever say what I needed to."

"Maybe he was afraid," the poet said.

"It was me who was afraid." I said. "Not to die—I didn't even squeak in the backseat when he nearly killed us, remember? I was afraid to face. . . ."

"Face what?"

I had no answer. The barman had slipped back in, and watching him glance at us sidelong, I thought of Ian Bailey, who'd once frequented this bar, having come to Ireland yearning for a home he'd never known. Was it his specter that paralyzed me? His words, stammered, revised, submitted to a poet, swallowed, finally congealed into a hammer propelled by madness. I knew his failure. Was I terrified of walking mute and outlawed in his shoes?

My father taught me everything except this: to converse with a Goddess and still keep a place inside that stays untouched.

And my father, in the guise of an Irish poet, slid my poem, marked with his cuneiform, across the table, saying, "You might make something of this."

Meaning not, as Phil Brady would have meant, a life. Meaning, I hope, a filament entwining words and world.

10.

INCARNATE

Sleep is lovely. Death is better still.
Not to have been born is of course the miracle.
—Heinrich Heine

Here's an outtake from *The Alice Crimmins Case* as my father told it.

Phil and Anne Brady sit in a gin mill on Northern Boulevard, across the table from Alice, dolled in her flame cocktail dress, who leans toward Joe Rorech—a bull in a cream suit with a wife and real-estate business on the Island. Dewers on the rocks for Phil, a Rusty Nail for Joe, gin-and-tonics for the girls.

The Mets' bonus baby, Eddie Kranepool, is finally starting to pay off, and Joe thinks he's the real deal.

"Sweet swing, this kid. Reminds me of Kiner," he says, waving an arc of cigar smoke over the table.

Alice pushes her chair back and taps Joe's cufflink. "Which way's the powder room," she purrs, and gives them a tilt of her beehive. Anne giggles. Phil points past the bar, crooks a finger left. Alice rises. Joe leans back, nooges her backside as her hips slink by.

In the foyer Alice pauses, toes a disk of gum on the floor tile, then turns right. She fishes in her purse for a dime and pinches it into the pay phone. "Hello, Eddie, it's me."

"Hey Baby, where are you?" Eddie Crimmins asks.

"Breslin's, with Anne and Phil."

"I'll be right over."

Alice hangs up, snaps her purse shut, drifts into the ladies' room, then floats back to the table, squeezing Joe's arm and tendering a freshly powdered cheek. Fifteen minutes later, when Alice's husband walks in, Phil spots him first. His back is turned—a block of plaid—and his black coif glistens as he scans the bar. No one moves until Joe slides down in his chair, slithers under the table. A tremor in the tablecloth, the back door swings, and he's gone. Bourbon in hand, Eddie saunters over and takes Joe's chair. No one looks away from the table. No one mentions the half-full cocktail at the empty place.

If English is a language, a people, a department, and a ball-spin, once, in the city of Lubumbashi in province of Shaba in the nation of Zaire, it was also an escape route. Thousands made their way there, slithering under tables on their way out the back door, fleeing the most implacable of husbands: Mobutu Sese Seko Kuku Benza Waza Banga (Mobutu, He, Himself: the Cock that Fears No One), President for Life. To escape being drafted into his ragtag army they came by boat, plane, truck, and bicycle to a bombed-out airport, rigged into a hedge school called UNAZA—Université Nationale du Zaire. All the best and brightest from forest and savanna crowded into Quonset huts, dreaming of acronyms: UN, CARE, AID, IMF, or else the black market that trafficked in diamonds, currency, electronics, and guns. By means of the English Department of UNAZA, I slithered under a table and out of the back door, disappearing from a job as dishwasher in Cork's Captain America's. Joining the Peace Corps, I dissolved from self-loathing, vanished from invisibility.

Shaba too was well underway in the process of disappearing, the whole province devolving from savanna to brick, brick to dust, animals to extinction, copper to Europe. What was left behind was haunted. Students slept in hangars. Marble from the grand colonial train station stubbed toes in the open-air marché.

Even the name "Shaba" was just a charm Mobutu had made up to quell the spirit of rebellion embodied in the province's real, forbidden name, "Katanga."

All morning, as the sun broiled the corrugated roof, I paced before benches of freshman reading aloud from books donated by the carton: the dross of Eng. Lit., anthologies with flyleaves inscribed "Ex Libris" or stamped "property of Madeford Co." We slogged through Shakespeare, Zane Gray, Hemingway, Poor Richard, and Whitman, swaying to the rhythms of distant times and places. In the afternoons I coached the basketball team, recruited from backbench cornhuskers. We practiced patterns scripted in Pocono summer camps where teens in official imitation NBA jerseys were doped up with the same fantasies that I peddled on this cracked asphalt court, except that here players ran barefoot, wearing shorts cut from burlap sacks, chanting through lay-up drills, "Lubumbashi oyé! UNAZA oyé!"

What was real and not going anywhere was La Cité, the suburb that ringed the old colonial town. It was a ghetto of clay and tin, palm oil and car skeletons, pulsing with music from tape decks in a hundred shebeens. Come Saturday night, a gaggle of bearded and beaded volunteers would pile into the Peace Corps jeep and bounce over roads that narrowed to paths, splashing through mud and foliage, swerving around chickens, pigs, and goats. Finally, rubbing knees and butts, we'd pour out of the jalopy into the courtyard of our favorite dive, Le Refuge, and there we danced. In candlelight and generator light we whirled to reggae and samba, the pagnes and abacosts all around us swaying in delicate syncopation, undulating as if an abrupt move might bruise the moonlight. For us, it was all elbows and hips, pivoting in space that always seemed too cramped. Our dance was kicks and grasps. But for the citoyens et citoyennes de La Cité, the dance was more. It lasted all night, and they paced themselves, eyes vacant, bodies held in a cylinder of air, each movement a deeper relaxation. It was a kind of knowing, their dance, a collaboration between holding and releasing, between being enfolded in a web and expressing the least nth of self. It was a dance performed at the last checkpoint before disappearing, and always in great numbers, its patterns unseen except maybe from rooftops or balconies. But there were no balconies;

this was La Cité in 1981, just three years after the province had erupted in flames and the town was evacuated and La Cité had choked with refugees and cholera.

This is how it had happened. At sunrise on June 6, 1978, with the taste of charred wood pungent in the air, farmers waved their arms, stumbling in from surrounding hills, and the mammas with babies slung across their backs in knotted cloth clapped shut the open-air marché and wrapped smoked fish, sombé, and manioc tubers in burlap. In a wave, it moved—the rumors, the fear—the Katangé were coming. Dust clouds appeared above the Kolwezi road; a caravan of trucks trundled up from the south. Soon you could hear them, "Katanga, oyé! Tshombé, oyé!" The call to the dead, the full-throated response from the army of the Katangé, the children of the regiments Mobutu had routed fifteen years before, returning to claim the province, its copper, myth, and malachite, gateway to Zambia and beyond. They swept through La Cité, devouring maize, pestles, tires, chickens, and machetes, surging toward the town, where government soldiers piled barricades and barked into two-way radios. Commerçants spaded jewels into their rose gardens; Mercedes clogged the road to the Zambian border.

We had heard the story in hushed tones from expats at the Greek Club—how the rebels used fetishes to make themselves invisible, how they routed Mobutu's army from the town, how finally the army—not the rebels—shot any whites they found on the streets so the UN would send mercenaries to intervene. And mercenaries had come: on June 9, professionals culled from the CIA Rolodex were flown in by Belgian transports. Within days they secured the town and rendered the rebels more invisible than any fetish could. Those were the rumors salting the air, resonating in the bass of the music that lured us to La Cité in Lubumbashi in 1981, after the smoke of the latest revolution had cleared.

"Evil Elizabethville"—that's what this town had been called before independence. To volunteers visiting from bush posts, its ramshackle two-story buildings held the allure of Paris. Cropped heads bandanna'd, they clambered down from trucks, their backpacks stuffed with cash and homegrown pot. They ogled fruit stands, gorged on bifsteak and samosas, and slugged down refrigerated Simba beer. The women passed afternoons in luke-warm baths leafing through *Time*; the men trolled bars. They came to restock supplies or to blow the stipends they couldn't spend en brusse. Some had been medevaced to Lubum to take the cure for amebic dysentery—a three-week regimen of cyanide tablets that killed the parasites and almost killed the human host. Whatever the mission, the high point of their visit was the marathon of dance and drink in La Cité. Most nights we were three: Reggie, Mike, and me, swaggering through the half-door into the courtyard of Le Refuge, with its bullet-pocked walls and plank bar.

Reggie was a Bed-Sty kid posted to a mission school up the Lualaba, so far out in the bush that his own voice spooked him. And not only his voice. At night there were the stars and pythons and mosquitoes; during the days he endured tsetse flies, nuns, sour palm wine, and chiggers, and always the exhausting vigilance: boiling water to brush his teeth, sweeping the out-house for spiders, picking worms from rice. There were the heat and stench and encompassing silences. When it was too much, Reggie would ditch school, flag down a pirogue, cross the river, and climb on a truck headed for Lubum. For twelve hours he'd squat in the open carriage with mamas and scabby kids, bellies bloated with kwashiorkor, looking like poster children from UNICEF ad campaigns—except the posters didn't show the flies and shit and rancid palm oil. All this for a few nights at Le Refuge. Here, decked out in high-collared taupe abacost with plump buttons, Reggie styled—shades low, chin high. He liked being taken for a local patron, as he was until he opened his mouth. Even after hearing his franglais, some still thought him Zairois, just faking. Other took him for a fetisheur.

Mike was a Georgia tackle who joined the Peace Corps to check out the Third World and teach shop. The trouble was that the school they sent him to had no electricity, so he passed his days playing Frisbee and teaching ESL. In the mornings he'd shamble into class to face the greeting he'd taught his mission pupils, "Wake up you fat old bull-e-dog," which they sang sweetly, thinking it a respectful salutation. Mike knew everyone and had managed to ingratiate himself with the American consulate, so he spent most nights house-sitting for diplomats, thawing TV dinners and watching videotaped football.

And there was Phil Brady in 1981: knock-kneed, pigeon-chested, with lopsided ears on a head two zip codes long. He could wolf down six eggs, sing like a Killarney jukebox, and jerk himself off into a swoon. What he couldn't know yet, being in Africa and invulnerable and capable of flight, was that inside him thrummed a passacaglia stronger than mind or will.

This he, I, was charged to find out. One night in La Cité, as I danced to music ratcheted to a fever pitch, a bottle of Simba glided toward me and tipped into the glass I held outstretched. Almost before I turned, it was gone. I glimpsed a halo of bright hair at eye level, three bodies off. Pale shoulders swiveled, a flame-red pagne melted into the flow. I couldn't follow, didn't have the words or legs or enough Simba. Instead I snaked through the courtyard to the jag of wall staked out by Reggie and Mike.

"You see that?"

Reggie shrugged. "A city full of gorgeous citoyennes, and you pick out the one msungu chick? Man, you should have stayed in Queens."

"That's La Belge," Mike said. "Tray fucked, mon frayre," and he guffawed. "But she is belle. Her husband's this old geezer who owns Aubegines—the four-star joint en ville. He's a gun-bare nutcase. Claims he fought in World War Two."

"La Belge." I waded back into the press of bodies. Her blonde aura moved and vanished and appeared again in the ebb and flow. Then all at once she was beside me, her lean form unfolding from the dance.

"Genevieve," she said, and the rest was lost in the blare of reggae and the explosive shock of her hand brushing against my arm.

Costumed in hollandaise wax pagne and halter top, she looked like a World's Fair figurine. Her braids spiraled around a teak hairpin, and on her throat she wore a bronze medallion—a trinket left behind by the Katangé. Her cheekbones made serene planes of her face; but when she looked right at me, her aqua eyes tensed, apprehending piecemeal, darting from my nose to neck to my maroon T-shirt with its washed-out arc of letters—FORDHAM.

She didn't dance like a msungu but moved in tune with that ever-so-slight time warp that slowed the earth's rotation, nights in La Cité, by an infinite fraction. She knew the code of élan—could do "La Canard," with a riff of bare shoulder, where the vaccination mark shone livid. With the least shift of her espadrilles she kept the beat, while her hips mimed ennui and her fingers dipped into the sliver of night between us. Msungu and Zairoise, she was an alembic of all that was absent here—Europe, America—and all I could not reach: the immutable present of La Cité.

My brain searched for a scrap of French—a phrase, a word—but I could say nothing. My shoulders and hips rolled, pastiching rhythm. She stayed, moving around me, working closer without word or touch, as I learned by doubling her gestures, my left arm frozen, holding the glass she had refilled. Toward dawn, when we started the trek home, Mike driving, Reggie slumped in front, so much had happened that it seemed natural that Genevieve lay curled beside me in the back, asleep.

Lubumbashi by night: the Wild West feel of it, dunes and giant anthills, clay boulevards lined with flamboyants and jacarandas. The sky was immediate, frangible, not smudged by smog or lights, and under it the whole city seemed poised to dissolve into savanna: elephant grass sprouting between buildings, dogs nosing garbage. Electricity was so spotty that recently a night flight had turned south to Zambia because the pilot couldn't find the airport. Here Lumumba had been murdered; here Tshombé had gone underground.

We turned onto Avenue de la Revolution, with its bazaar signs painted in French, Greek and Arabic, then sped past the carrefour's plaster stanchion, where soldiers milled around smelt fires and brandished rifles at passing cars—unloaded, Mike claimed. We lumbered down the long hill past the Japanese golf course to the European district, where diplomats and engineers from Gecomines lived in tracts of ranches guarded by sentries sleeping behind walls topped with glass shards and razor wire.

"Kasavubu Street," she'd said when she climbed into the jeep, and Mike knew the place. "The Ponderosa," he called it, a pink hacienda at the end of a winding avenue.

We rolled up before the locked gates, and I squeezed her arm, felt her wake. She sat up, flexed her neck. Then she clasped my shoulders and fitted the plane of her cheek to my cheek, and while I was still puckered, grazed the other cheek, completing a maneuver few Americans have mastered. She shimmied down from the gashed rumble seat and stood facing me in the gravel drive in halter and pagne. Maybe she waved; maybe it was just a look. Maybe it was the fact of her standing still for the first time, silhouetted under a eucalyptus before the iron gate spancilled with kudzu. She looked so frail that she shimmered; tendrils floating from the teak hairpin, sandals dangling from her pinky.

When the jeep reversed, wiggling up the drive, I found myself beside her, watching the back of Mike's neck craning to follow the curve, his shoulders shaking as he gave Reggie a poke. Genevieve rattled the gate, and a tiny, bent sentry gripping a kerosene lamp shuffled out, calling, "Jambo, Madame." She took my hand, and we walked down the gravel path to the back door, unlocked, then tiptoed through the kitchen into the dark living room, where Genevieve flipped a switch, illuminating a plush sofa and glass coffee table and beige carpet and a sand painting bought at the marché and framed as if the scene it depicted were a thousand miles off. Stepping back far enough for me to see all of her, she said in English, "I am married." Then she crossed her arms over her belly, peeled the ruffled halter over her breasts, unknotted her pagne, and stood before me in a flame red pool of cloth.

Until that moment I had never disappeared while standing still, all my vanishing having taken place by flight—Queens to Ireland to Africa—and as for love, the little I'd known hadn't involved vaporizing. Before, love had meant a presence backlit by fantasy. I'd felt its pleasure, shared vistas, two walking together shoulder to shoulder, and nights lying entwined down the body's length. In love, as in dance in La Cité, I'd come to the last checkpoint before disappearing, but had always been held back. Now, in this ersatz living room with its malachite ashtrays and gold-leaf lampshades, I was gone.

Easy to claim now, in middle age in Ohio, that Genevieve and Shaba and Joe Rorech vanished into history. Why be surprised that a young man sharing with me a name and half a life was overcome while making love with the tuneful, long-limbed body of a woman who came from so far off it might as well have been another planet? A Belgian married to a hero of the Resistance, living in Africa. She opened her lean thighs, bit my earlobe, reached behind and teased the hairs on the inner slopes of my buttocks. One maverick mosquito shared our blood. Does that sound like disappearing?

But when an incarnation is trapped in a vortex of time and space, and pressure is exerted from furniture and morning and covenants and the unfathomable mind with its need to link instant to instant in a chain, that incarnation is quickly depleted of visibility. Flesh may resist, may lunge at the nearest flesh— caress, lick, knead, penetrate—to stay corporeal. But the harder it fights, the faster the body fades, not into love or history but into the disappearing moment.

It was mid-morning before I rematerialized and propped myself up on an elbow. Strewn around us were pants, a pagne, shoes, wine bottles, a maroon shirt. I touched the incarnation next to me, and she opened brilliant eyes, looked up at the ceiling, then turned on her back and lit a cigarette. Below her belly button, a livid, stitched scar emerged from the blonde tuft of hair.

"What is this?" I asked, tracing the line.

She turned her face away. "This is my lost child."

At Alice Crimmins' trial, the prosecution called Joe Rorech to testify against his former lover. His real-estate deals were coming apart; the cops leaned on him, and he folded. In court he declared that, late one night in her apartment, after meeting for drinks at Breslin's on Northern Boulevard, Alice had poured out her heart, confessed her guilt, sobbing, "I did it. I killed them, Joe." The courtroom erupted. Alice covered her face; finally she wept in public.

That night—the night in question—did Joe Rorech disappear? Was this betrayal in open court meant to recover his wholeness, including wife and children and friends and business? In order to remain visible, he had to account for the entire evening, not just the Rusty Nails and the detective and his perky wife and the ex-husband appearing out of nowhere. So when he came to the disappearing act, did he write himself an outtake?

Let's say that after leaving Breslin's, Joe Rorech doesn't go straight home. He's angry, steaming. He drives around, from Northern Boulevard over to Francis Lewis, to Kissena Park, where little Eddie's corpse had been found, back to Northern. Without meaning to, he winds up back in front of the neon shamrock in Breslin's plate-glass window. He parks under a streetlight, and waits until finally Alice comes out of the front door with Anne and Phil, the doltish husband skulking behind. It's a calm summer evening with bright stars. They loiter a few moments under the green awning, then the Bradys drift off, and Alice and Eddie move toward their separate cars. Joe slinks down till Alice's Ford glides out of the parking lot. He follows her home and wheedles his way in and holds her on the sofa as she weeps, confesses.

Joe Rorech declared all this in open court. He'd been stunned, he said. He'd always believed her story—how she'd checked the kids at 3 o'clock, didn't miss them till the next morning. He told the court that when Alice sobbed, "I killed them, Joe; forgive me," he'd gotten up from the sofa and left immediately, had never spoken to Alice after that night. Fully himself again, he announced to a gallery of fellow citizens that he'd abandoned his lover because she'd murdered her children. Maybe he believed his tale. How else to go on? In a courtroom packed with witnesses there was no table to slide under.

Here I testify, only a blue screen for witness, to disappearing not just one moment but many. During the days I taught, played hoops, and drank Simba with Mike and Reggie at some downtown joint. But at night, instead of driving to La Cité, I pedaled my big red Peace Corps bike to Aubergines, where Genevieve played hostess. I took a bar stool and ordered Pernod, squinting in the cigarette smoke, trying to follow a thread of the patois.

He liked me—Arpad, Genevieve's husband—so he said. Americans, yes, he liked Americans. No matter what others said. Why I came to sit with these Belgians, he did not ask. He planted himself at the crotch of the big oak-paneled bar, scanning the dining room with its imported chandeliers and gleaming appointments and Zairois waiters in bow ties. He was old, sixty perhaps, but old enough, I wondered, to have fought in World War Two? His balding pate was mottled with brown stains, his teeth were filmy, and his tortoiseshell glasses bulged his taupe eyes.

His young wife flitted from the bar to the kitchen to the

dining room, or sat with us, smoking Gauloises. She did not smile or speak. She drank Pernod or brandy or Passport scotch, never looking my way, but sometimes in the bar mirror I saw her eyes tense, as he told, in guttural French, episodes from a story whose point eluded me.

Always there was snow. I think he was saying "blizzards," and once, fingering my short sleeve, he said, "like this." Summer uniforms. They hadn't expected to fight into the winter. Many things happened. Many things were done. Terrible things. But I didn't know the Resistance even had uniforms. Dogs collared with explosives were trained to crawl under tanks. "Poof," Arpad said, his thumb pushing a button. Troops lived on garbage, slept in the carcasses of horses, warming themselves by fires made from the artillery caissons. In a factory by a river, fighting was so horrible that the armies were piled up on different floors like sandwiches. He laced his thick fingers. And he, a boy, terrified, on the roof, in the snow, with the stench of burning in his nostrils.

Listening to him, I saw only a scar on my lover's belly.

On the days when Arpad traveled, I biked down the long avenue to the Ponderosa. Whole mornings lay before us, too long to spend on bliss. Afterwards, we played house, sitting half-naked at the Formica kitchen table, smoking, sipping coffee, chatting in franglais. She was from Liege but did not love waffles. She had not been good in school. She did not care. I mimed my preening before students, made her laugh. I sipped boiled coffee from a Delft cup and asked why she had married Arpad.

"My father," she said, taking a drag on her cigarette and gazing out the window.

He was a drunken man—her father—and he beat her. When she was sixteen, she ran away. Became pregnant. The boy did not know, would not care. She laughed, shrugged. She wanted the infant. She found Arpad, an old friend of the family, like an uncle. But Genevieve always knew, had seen in the tiny eyes that he wanted to be more than uncle, even when she was a child. Arpad arranged all, brought her here, to Katanga.

"Did Arpad meet your father in the Resistance?" I asked.

This made her laugh too. Did I wonder, she asked, about the uniforms? And the dogs and the snow?

"He is Flemish, you know," she told me. "You understand,

73

many of the Flemish did not mind so much when the Germans came. Some joined. This is how he saw so much of the snow. One does not read of this."

"And the scar?" I asked.

The procedure. The doctors here, *incompétents*. The infant was born dead, had to be cut out. She became sick, for months. Now she can never have children. And the lost one haunts.

My father once held Alice Crimmins in his arms. "They're dead, they're dead," she wailed, rocking back and forth. In the basement, the tape recorder whirred; upstairs, a boy pressed his face between the banister rails.

Though he'd been assigned to entrap, my father erased the tapes made in his basement. Why? It's unlikely, with detectives eavesdropping, that the recordings incriminated Alice. Perhaps they incriminated my father—his whispered "there, there's" betraying feelings that went deeper than sympathy for a traduced suspect. Why else would he hand over to her lawyer, as I learned from *The Alice Crimmins Case*, tapes proving that under police pressure the coroner had changed the time of death to contradict Alice's 3 a.m. alibi? Was the thrum inside him stronger than he knew? Did it make him betray the code binding him to the Police Force, to his wife, to Queens, to the world he'd known? Or perhaps that thrum pulsed from another source beneath code and pledge: from a yearning to cleave to the truth as he saw it. Maybe he was still bent on straightening things out.

And what of my role in the story? Were it not for *The Alice Crimmins Case*, whose author based his theory of Alice's innocence on long interviews with my father, I would have been enveloped in the silence he faced in every cop bar and squad room till his early retirement. I would not have understood the abrupt end to the catalogue of clippings nor have known that he hated Frank Serpico for fear of being seen in the same light. Without that book, I'd have only a memory of a fanciful pater-familias who in 1966 announced at the dinner table that he was chucking his job for a new post in a Brooklyn themed in mystery.

In spite of books and records, my tale felt true, immersed as I was in a perfection of memory like Mary's, lulled by a thrum—

maybe the Goddess's pulse—rhythm and repetition kneading words into flesh, flesh into characters. The tale kept me spellbound, shielding me from that unknowable universe, my father.

The morning Arpad walked in on us, it was not because Genevieve had dropped a dime, as Alice had. The sentry probably tipped him off. Yet we knew the time was coming, could feel ourselves becoming more visible day by day. And Genevieve must have wanted to be seen, as Alice had, calling her husband from a pay phone to surprise her lover. And Arpad too—he must have longed for Genevieve to bear witness to the German uniform under his skin.

Hordes of the betraying and betrayed close in around me this evening in Ohio: real-estate tycoons vanishing under tablecloths, Belgians howling on Russian rooftops, dancers bedecked with souvenirs from the Katangé, the corpses of two children found in Queens. I wave, still trying to shape them, the way wisps of cigar smoke once conjured the arc of Eddie Kranepool's home-run swing.

PART THREE

BAUCIS

When at last
In frail old age they stood before
The temple's door and spoke of years gone by,
Philomen saw Baucis shake green leaves around her,
And she herself saw Philomen wear leaves.
Around their faces branches seemed to tremble,
And as bark climbed their lips as if to close them,
They cried, "Farewell, good-bye, dear wife, dear husband."

—OVID

11.

BAUCIS, STRANDED

You have taken the east from me; you have taken the west from me; you have taken what is before me and what is behind me; you have taken the moon, you have taken the sun from me; and my fear is great that you have taken God from me!

—LADY GREGORY

In June 1994, after four strokes and liver cancer, my father died, and Pet had nowhere to go. 53-28 was sold, Mirror Lake was a luxurious prison. There was no east or west, she could not disappear or change into a tree like Baucis and Philomen, though if one of the truants my father cuffed or a clerk in the Board of Ed secretary pool had been Zeus disguised, perhaps my parents, born in the same month in the same year and married for more than half a century, would have petitioned to entwine. But there was no tree, nothing to hold or to grow into, so she flew west to visit me in Sausalito, where I lived in a colony of New Age artists.

There was the Swedish artist who made wedding dresses from soiled underwear, placing ads in the *Bay Guardian* and receiving fat packages daily. There was the artist in a wet suit constructing an abalone shell installation in the surf. There was the hip-hop artist, and the East German gyration hypnotists. There was the Lakota storyteller who made English glance back troubled over its shoulder, and there was me: a cherub trying to herd a pageant of ghosts into frail stanzas. We lodged in converted officers' barracks horseshoeing a glade with a postcard view of the San Francisco Bay.

Tonight in Ohio, I think of Pet's westbound flight to join me. Outside, the wind raged, the jet's skin tensing against freezing air, but inside, Pet tacked in dream toward her firstborn, with no destination other than the one memory navigated.

I would like to explain death, to say, "Take note. This is how it is accomplished." But I haven't the heart. I can't fly direct, any more than Pet could fly to join my father. My blood still coils as purposefully as headlights through fog, keeping to the paths and knitting the paths together, and blood kept me from joining my mother on her return flight. So, like a movie sleuth hoofing down a backstreet after a shadow, glomming my fedora, trenchcoat's wings aflap, I pull up sharp at the butt of a blind alley. I shuffle around for clues, sullen, but relieved the shadow hadn't turned. Already the blood cools, the mouth goes cotton, and even as I step over a white feather wilting in the gutter, the chase crystallizes into language, flattening to a coin I snap down on the cherrywood bar, ready to regale cronies. I check out my hairline in the saloon mirror. Someone smooths a buck for the jukebox. Pull up a stool, pal. Just the facts.

I awaited Pet's arrival in the lounge of San Francisco International's last terminal, big as a Roman arena, lined with bistros and souvenir shops. The surrounding gates opened on cities, releasing dribbles, then packs, of joint-sore newbies. Some were plucked out with squeals and hugs; others humped their carry-ons through the barrier, straightening, becoming local with every step.

When the Ozymandian voice of Delta intoned "New York," I shifted on my bar stool, holding back: how fast could an old woman deplane? But by the time I had signed for my scotch and sidled up to the velvet banister, she was already up the ramp, first off, listing in a wheelchair guided by a skycap, parting the swell of wayfarers. And there she was, lacking only a bang and cobalt smoke to make me think she'd materialized from the tunnel by magic.

What do you tip for the delivery of your mother? I grabbed one handle, but the skycap wouldn't give. He grinned in kinship or complicity, his dimples winking, and for a few steps we scuffled and butted, the wheelchair rudderless. Finally the powers of the air released her for a crumbled five, and I leant down, felt her sour breath, and kissed her back to earth.

Until that moment I'd never felt alone with Pet. Although she'd nursed and bathed and fed me, shopped with me, picked me up at school, and made trips to the beach, throughout my childhood my father's presence had loomed, sparing only a few memories of his absence. There was the afternoon after school when Pet and I had sat at the kitchen table while stew bubbled on the stove, passing the time before dinner deciphering my hand gibberish. Squeezing my palms together, I'd pressed the tips of my index fingers back until the joints splayed into a roof, then peered inside, conjuring a creature dwelling untouchable beneath the flesh archway.

"Don't make a house," Pet had smiled, unknotting my fingers. Then she taught me her code: three squeezes on the knuckles— "I love you;" two back—"Me too."

And there was the afternoon I'd run all the way home from Tommy Knapp's third-grade gynecological fantasy. I flew upstairs, trapped Pet in the bathroom. "Show me," I demanded.

"Ah you whelp, I can't, I'd be ashamed." But she consented to tell, and her description: a matted pinprick hole too small to see, made my father's explanation seem savage. Her fable thwarted years of groping.

One summer afternoon, home from college and bored, I tempted Pet down into the basement for a glimpse into the rebellion their tuition dollars paid for. I read aloud Bukowski's *Burning in Water, Drowning in Flame*, savoring each "fuck" and "shit," then unwrapped an ornate bong and demonstrated as if it were a wonder of science, explaining carburetor and filtration. But even as she giggled out wisps of pungent smoke, her eyes darted north. He was never wholly gone.

In later years, on my visits home, Pet and I would huddle in the kitchen with highballs after a day of jumping to my father's stuttering demands, soothing him, bandaging the oozing toe, swabbing the eye he'd blinded falling out of bed when the hospital released him after a stroke.

"I j-just, I just slipped. In the bathroom," he'd repeated till they'd freed him. Name and rank. Whatever you say, say nothing. Even in her sleep his presence pinched her earlobe, his decaying gravity somehow tightening her orbit.

Now, for the first time, in the San Francisco airport in 1994, he was gone. Maneuvering through the crowd with mincing steps, I asked about the chair. Pet half-turned, her lips' rictus warning that already her flesh had started casting off.

"Special service, you know. I'm walking fine. A few slips only. Aren't I the queen and the queen mum."

And so she was. Though her life had been molded like playdough, though she'd never touched the TV remote control, though Francis McCann had called her "daughter" right up to his deathbed so as not to be bothered remembering four girls' names, tonight as our wheels divided walkway traffic, she was, for the first time, a feeble star.

Her queries: "Why are the hills brown? Is there good bread here? Bagels? There's nowhere like New York for steaks, is there? What would sailing be like? Fishing? Are there Irish in San Francisco? Have you met nice girls?"

We cruised over the bridge and climbed the winding mountain road overlooking the Bay, smothered now in a fog that snuffed all light outside the dashboard's radium. Arriving at the colonnade of eucalyptus, we entered the huge hall where the artists met nightly for feasts of fennel and goat cheese, tofu decorated-as-duck, broccoli pizza, sombé, blackened salmon.

And afterwards, exhibits and performances. The rafts of tube lights blinked out; sitar music swelled; an ouroboros coalesced from fragments of math equations on a screen that shivered like a sail. Next, spotlights searched the stage and froze two garish togas. Spinning, writhing, and jousting with fluorescent sticks, they pantomimed what the program called "Resistance/Sex: A Kabuki Drama." For the finale, a dreadlocked figure rose from the back row and pointed a remote at the projector wired to the rafters. On the screen erupted images of flame, cars smoldering, smoke billowing over an LA cityscape. In a rumbling voice, the artist began interpreting the spools and hieroglyphs chalked all over the sawdust floor, instructing us to contemplate the cosmology of heaven and hell. We were an African village, he told us. We were witnesses. We were ghosts. All the while I stole glances at Pet, who sat listless, touching her glasses' bridge as if watching a parade of TV sitcoms.

Later, in her Bay-view hotel room, sprawled under her bed canopy, slurping forbidden gin from plastic cups, she said how strange it had all been. Not strange that I was here on the edge of the wrong ocean rubbing shoulders with artists; I'd always been strange that way.

"It happens in America sometimes," she sighed. "Comes of mixing: bourbon, Bushmills; Brooklyn, Belfast," a laugh. Why was her son born like this? she wondered. Had she been ravished by a pooka? Or was it just that they had both been nearing forty, had been trying to make me for two decades, had almost given up.

"Maybe we prayed too hard, were heard in the wrong place— the riot instead of the village." Her wicked grin. "Changeling, we'd say. RH factor, said the doctors."

I'd been born blue as if I'd run from a far place, was saved by cartons of American blood, and since then I'd been druidish, bad-hearted; always hunched at the hi-fi rocking, or crying to play ball, or stringing after some harpy. Had there been Special Ed, I would have been in it. She knew; she'd seen them, poor things, at the Board. That's how it was in America—not strange, really; there was nothing to do about it.

What was strange was being so looked at. Sitting at the head of the huge slab of a dinner table—the questions, the looks. And after the lights hummed on and my turn to perform had come, I'd led her by the elbow up to a seat in the first row, freckles exposed, then mounted the plywood steps to the podium and introduced her to the artists, telling how the McCanns had landed in America, how seventy years later I'd chauffeured Pet and Aunt Mary for a shopping trip to Brooklyn, and after dropping them on Court Street and circling to park, I'd spotted them on the sidewalk, and for an instant my sight pierced time's veil, and this pair of crones clutching shopping bags against the century's onslaught were transfigured into two girls creeping hand in hand through Moloch's palace, and after packing Pet and

Mary into the backseat and strong-arming traffic onto the BQE, I'd asked what it had felt like all those years ago.

"We were dead scared, son," Mary'd replied, suddenly cogent, "with the tall buildings and all the people. But what was more, what was the most strange, was they told us, son, that underneath the city there was another city." The subways. That's how it must have seemed.

And I wrote a poem to the weird brood, sent it to Pet, who'd said on the phone, "It's perfect," swelling my heart, until she added, "Not a single typo." Her secretary years. A ripple of laughter from the artists, more looks pincushioning her. As she sat with hands folded, I raised my head, shut my eyes, and launched into "First Born."

Later that night, leaning toward her under the mauve bed tent in the hotel, I asked her, "Did you mind, Pet? Did you like it?"

"I liked some of it. Some of the artists."

"Did you mind the poem? Did you like my poem?"

"It, well . . . it made me feel small, and large at the same time, a bloated leprechaun." She laughed, sighed.

It was this air, the atmosphere gone anemic in my father's absence. Words distended, burst, could get no purchase on the ear. He went without a sign, and she felt betrayed. Why didn't he speak, gesture? He was sick, yes, to death. The strokes had hit him over and over like lightning that didn't know it had just one shot at a target, changing him, turning his face, drowning, spinning him around toward her, away, always corkscrewing down away from the world. Toward the end he'd faced straight on where he was headed. Then cancer. A year with chemo, six months without.

"Whatever Pet wants," he'd breathed, exhausted, waving as if turning down a second helping, passing it to her, the huge, cold dish.

And after the first treatment he was gone. He'd been facing away so long, still grabbing for her, facing and turning away and she was always there, feeling him dwindle, rummaging the slivers of him for some ember, anything the strokes had not burnt out. And she was there, in the hospital after the chemo, holding his hand. She hadn't even known. His absence.

But now she felt it—helium dizziness, gravity zeroed out. The untrustworthy air tattooed her pupils; her left ear wouldn't hold her glasses straight and sometimes she fell. And the looks that he would have shielded with his presence—with his presences, for he was fey and could take several forms: his jokester presence that sent all the needles spinning, or the priestly one that wouldn't suck an egg, or the Achillean one, bilious with dark virtue. Now she had to absorb all the looks herself.

And in the hours after he'd gone silently, she couldn't speak— couldn't tell me, made Brian call me in California. Maybe her love engorged her, trapping her memory in a hospital, but it was another hospital: the one where I'd lain as an infant—a blue doll sealed in a sterile case, quilled with tubes, laboring with my blood. And my father, draped over her steel bed rail, crying and crying. "There, there," she'd smoothed his hair.

"He loved that one so," she sobbed, "his first," clutching my brother. And so she'd flown toward me.

I kissed her asleep after midnight in the hotel in Sausalito, and when I returned the next morning I found her wedged between bed and night table, her face mottled, right arm seizing, her bare chest spasming like a wounded moth.

12.

PARDON, OLD FATHERS

They have learning of their own, but I pass their learning by.
What can they know, that we know, that know the time to die?

—W. B. Yeats

and hatch the still unborn wing
of the night, sister
of the orphaned wing of the day,
that is not really a wing since it is only one.

—Cesar Vallejo

When she woke after three days, and the doctors extubated her and untaped her lips, Pet had gone so far toward perfection of memory that my father lived. How would he be told about all this? He was upset so easily these days. Prompted, she'd return to now, to me.

"Pet, he's dead."

"Yes, three weeks ago, I know," her voice hoarse. She shifted in and out, surfacing, sinking, the morphine like ram's blood drawing the starved dead. She welcomed each witnessing ghost, raising her plastic-braceleted arm, babbling, "a bushel and a peck, and a hug around the neck," her wide eyes darting in REM sleep. But the night when I'd left her in the hotel—that was vanished: the artists, the screen, the village, the riot, the poem, the fall. Had she spent all night spasming on the floor? Had she fallen just before I knocked? I wasn't there to see her cross wingless to the impossible space roofed by praying fingers. I don't know how she did it, and I can't bring her back as I drift worldward.

So the hospital engulfed her. *Hospital*, with its hint of pity, hospitality, with its foreboding echo—even the word deceives. They are not buildings, though they appear as a profusion of plaster and glass, coke machines, elevators, split levels, fire doors with leaded windows, a whiff of ammonia, green-badged personnel. You move through halls clutching flowers or the string of a platinum heart balloon, scuffing checked tiles, following painted arrows and sequenced numbers like a piece on a Parcheesi board. The recesses on either side—the curtains opening into exhibits of pain—register faintly, the way banks of caged tunnel lamps tighten the straphanger's squint as the train speeds past.

Nor are they staging areas, though if you draw near, become involved, hospitals exude controlled mayhem, with their procedures and operations, their codes and geodesic command centers, their war maps of the human systems—the skeleton, the nerves, the muscles, the bloodstream. And though there is no map of soul, never mind the soul's escape route, nurses starch out panic, computers dilate, specialists tap clipboards; the radar sweeps far.

And if you're hunched forward on a plastic chair, waiting for word, it can seem that hospitals are eyes peering into the just-before, the just-after. The machines, the codes, buildings seem constructed to observe the joining and unjoining of flesh and spirit. Birth, of course, is easy to track. You glance at the bovine husband sitting across the way, flipping through *Vogue*; for months he's watched, helpless. Even his slow gaze will not miss this. In those cases when the incarnation flutters and the infant comes too soon or comes, panting, from a far place, hospitals are ready: they enshrine the woad thing in a crystal sphere, and the eyes gleam. Death is more slippery, often missed. Still, hospitals are not eyes.

Had she been able to speak, my mother would have resisted the building and its combat zone and the eyes, her eyes having witnessed many times, from my unstrangling to my father's strokes, the aspects of hospitals. Had she been able to speak, there would have been, perhaps, no need to resist. Instead, for three days, the hospital became vast space, a curved continuum, Escher staircases. It became storms roiling overhead, then threading down, funneling into her mouth, her Belleek heart, her seizing brain.

The moment I touched the hotel telephone, she was theirs. The ambulance found me lying with her in the hotel room, fingering gibberish—love's CPR—as the room changed weather. Though they presented dutiful faces, the ambulance driver and crew looked like Queens boys, T-shirts stretched over bellies, forearms huge as tree boles. They barked signals into crackling radios, fiddled with straps, spun valves on machines big as Cadillac grills. Comically earnest, they worked so hard to keep the slouch out of their brawn, the cigarette sneer from their lips, that my nerves turned to them like plants to muted sunlight, craving to desert, go AWOL, jump ship and barhop back toward life.

But the pall separating Pet from us also cowled me from them. Even as the driver flicked on the siren and pulverized traffic lights by touching a green button on a black box, the chasm between us widened. At the hospital's ranch entrance he nodded me out, then backed to the side, where the crew trundled Pet's stretcher up the ramp, spiriting her back into a tunnel where I could not follow. So I sat on the front stoop, gazed across Marin, the rich crescent result of America. Nestled on the low hills amidst palms and eucalyptus, the slant-roofed villas awoke in dowels of light.

It is possible to change many things, but the things most worth changing won't budge. At twenty-four, magically delivered into the savanna of Zaire, drunk, in love with Genevieve, I'd lain spread-eagled near midnight in a swath of elephant grass, and it had hit me that this would not last. *This*, not meaning life: that would last; death was eons off. But this joy, this alignment of stars and cells—already, as soon as it filled me, it eluded me. Already the palm wine swamped the gourd of my skull, unkiltered the equatorial sky. However far I fled, the stars mapped no escape. Not travel, not relativity, not cryogenics—nothing would freshen the ichor or reveal the pattern of the cresting and troughing in my skyish veins. I'd followed dawn, followed my transfused blood. I would follow blindly, farther; follow now.

For three days I perched on a rolling stool next to my mother's gurney, following the rise and dip of numbers as mysterious as Dow Jones. Singing failed; so too touch, memory. When the nurses dusted me out, I rushed to the pay phone and disgorged everything to my brother, who went animal-mute with rage.

Each night I bent over the steel rail, kissed her, stroked her hair, whispering good-night, good-bye, as if she were asleep, more tenderly than if she were asleep and might awaken startled. She was a cipher, a lukewarm sculpture, her past opaque. Maybe, as the Chinese believe, her spirit wandered, needing a map back. But back where? Intensive Care, Marin General, California. Hearing that address, what wraith would cock an ear?

Each morning, I drove down the winding path from the colony, the Bay shimmering, the Golden Gate standing in defiance of a million snapshots. Then on through the rainbow tunnel, up California 5, the big-shouldered highway that promised Napa, Point Reyes, wine. I pulled in to Bhutti Boutari's 7-Eleven for flavored coffee, then veered left up Sir Francis Drake to Marin General, parked in a sliver of shade, frisked the seats for smokes, and marched up the steps and through the beautifully appointed lobby—familiar now: the gray-faced attendant at his desk, the blonde in the gift shop who made change while cradling a phone against her tanned cheek. A *Chronicle* from the cage and I was ready to take the visitors' elevator to the second floor and supplicate from the nave for permission to enter Intensive Care. This went on for lifetimes, for three days, and would go on, until finally, one morning, she was awake, accusation burning in her eyes, her right hand clawing its strap. I unknotted the cloth, and her arm with its plastic amulet floated upward. Her fingers found her mask, tapped it, signing her three beats: take it out.

"It wasn't me," I mouthed, wanted to blurt, but instead I promised, lied, rushed out of the room as frantic as Raskolnikov. Because it *was* me, had been from the first.

After the ambulance boys wheeled my mother into the tunnel, I'd pushed through the revolving door into the lobby. Inside, a pastel and a tweed suit had approached, spoken my name—mine alone now. They'd ushered me to a windowless paneled office and sat me on a beige love seat while they arranged armchairs. On the wall was a sailboat print; the fake oak coffee table was littered with new magazines. No one worked here; it was a room meant to contain, to muffle.

I thought, "Priests?" and my heart sank. Ministers? No collars: just black turtleneck and jaundiced tie. Coffee? A phone? Anything they could do? Voices soapy with professional respect. A moony face fringed with goatish beard, and the sidekick, silent, angular, an aging Dedalus. Their forms fibrillated as if missing a dimension. The moonface droned about recovering loss. He knew my feelings, quoted Gibran. The other stayed quiet, skeptical. I wanted to reach across the stilted air and rip out their spleens. They knew this, but kept puppeting. Who could murder in a vestibule?

"Thanks so much for your help," I'd said. "Can I see my mother now?"

"The doctor's coming soon. They're working on her."

Minutes, counted like a pulse. Then he arrived—slim, tanned, miles too young. Respectful silence, even from the priests.

He didn't know yet, no one knew, it might be anything, needed time to test, to stabilize—a breathing tube—and from me, a signature—permission. I was the son.

The words incomprehensible. But I'd signed and was released into emergency, where I tore the curtain open and saw the machine that wheezed under a grove of coat hangers slung with gleaming sacks, saw her arms strapped and her bloated face taped shut.

That night, driving back to Sausalito, I realized that we in the colony were nothing—just sprites. The doctors were the muscled seraphim, anointed with money and blood by a science that had swatted heaven flat. Every morning I trailed one or another of them—the internist, the cardiologist, the surgeon, the technician, the therapist, touching my forelock, "If you please, sir, such a slight miracle," my voice girlish. Each afternoon my fantasies titrated until I half believed the poison I poured over the phone into my brother's ear: the high-brow confab, what I'd told them, what they told me.

Once a doctor pivoted in his loafers, leveled his stare, "I can explain again what I told you yesterday if you need." Again, the blood-surge. Many had cringed before him with clenched fists.

"No, thank you very much."

But the truth is that I knew nothing, and my mother did not know when to die, though she knew how.

Old Father Yeats might pardon us, as he pardoned his country-men—the way they can't finish, the way they buttonhole the air after the listener flees; he blessed them, once, with his high hat, though he later recanted. "A lyric temperament," he intoned, "disdainful of drama." Nothing Nordic, no ending left unspoiled.

Eighty years later, hunched before a frazzling screen in April, my aunt dozing, muttering on the couch, I still can't end, can bind no knot. The words fade, yield meaning, blur again, the way my Pet clawed back, faded, spluttering with pneumonia, returning long enough to speak, to learn again to swallow, walk, to talk with ghosts.

Her observations: she liked morphine. She would not be intu-bated again, forbade it. Nothing, when your time came, was worth this. Her father and mother had passed this down. They were near. Listen.

Dying in my bedroom at 53-28, my grandmother hadn't understood the technology of the intercom, thought Pet spoke through walls. What my father went through—my mother understood that now. When I cried, I only got her wet. All the beloved dead were swarming, just out of ken. She would see them soon. This I should pass down. And when she died, again I was not there, was downstairs on the patio, smoking. "I'll be right back, Pet," I'd cooed, as if she heard. Was it my leaving let her go? Maybe she needed privacy to disinter the fetish she'd buried in the other world.

"It's for him," she whispered to the gathering crowd, "I've stayed this long for him," thumbing toward the door, rolling her eyes to the ghosts, who grasped, welcoming, as soon as I slipped out. For me she had endured the food, the pain, the second, the third intubation. I was so fragile, a changeling, had to be han-dled carefully. But I was gone now, she could go.

Or perhaps she left still buttonholing air.

And when for the last time I walked out of the sliding glass door of Marin General, where the landscaped gardens and immaculate interiors assure that nothing horrible can happen, I had missed everything and I was lighter by one wing.

OISIN

*Who would have thought the afterlife would
look so much like Ohio?*

—MAGGIE ANDERSON

NOT KNOWING,
RELYING ON INTUITION

Often I am permitted to return to a meadow,
Which is a scene made up in the mind,
Which is not mine, but is a made place

—ROBERT DUNCAN

ON Sundays Mary sits by the fire, her pulse ratcheted by TV sports. "Oh, look at all the people," she says. "Ach, he shouldn't have done that."

Now she slowly lifts her arms after a touchdown, astounding me, until I see that she only wants the melted ice cream napkined from her fingers.

It is April; a year has passed. Maybe Mary is starting to feel certain her new refuge won't collapse, even though the town around it is rubble. It might even outlast her, this mansion hulking on the main street of ex-steel barons, now devoted to processing deaths of those who remain behind, including Mary Martin, who's a veteran of being left.

On Sundays I enter the manor's smoggy foyer and weave among the wheelchairs down a linoleum tunnel, passing fritzed-out dreamers. And there she is, asleep in her gurney under the picture of the young McCann girls—Betty and Kay in plaid, Pet in baby twill, and Mary, shadowing behind them with a hand on Pet's shoulders, herding all of the goodly company of the dead. When I touch her shoulder, her aged face tilts and her arms float up for a touchdown.

"Are you taking me out, son? That's nice. They're a bit wild here you know, son. I thought they were quiet, *Protestants*"—she whispers the word—"but they're wild, son, even at night. Look at that ould one," and she points to the shrouded figure rocking back and forth. Mary doesn't bother to learn her room-mates' names. Some nights they leave and don't come back.

I sign her out, and Mary smirks at the starched nurse. "This is my boyfriend," she cackles.

"Well, isn't that just fine. Now you behave yourself out there, Mary," the nurse says, wagging her finger. "What's your boyfriend's name?" she asks.

Silence. After a moment, "He's my boyfriend. . . . Gorgeous," she offers.

I wheel her out to my car, lift her to her legs on the pavement, crack her chair's spine and heave it into the trunk. I guide her bird steps into the bucket seat and drive down the boulevard they call "5th Avenue"—though there's no Lexington or Park—right past my old apartment on the way to a new house. This is our Sunday, our return to a home Mary might believe is Brooklyn. "Will Flip be there?" she asks.

"No, Aunt Mary," I say. "Surprise! I'm Flip." And I flash her a toothy grin.

"Ach, of course. Flip was always the scholar. Brian was gorgeous. Flip was the scholar. Will we visit him?"

"Sure, Aunt Mary, someday."

"And is your mother there?"

"You'll see Pet soon enough."

We pull into the driveway between the holly hedge and bud-ding rose bush, and I wrestle the wheelchair out and take Mary under her arm—surprised at the good, thick, muscular flesh.

"Ach, this is a big parlor, son. It's like a dance hall. The paint's very clean. Do you have a girl to clean?"

"Not yet, Aunt Mary."

"If I'm not too fresh," and she gives a wheedling smile, "Did you get a bargain on it? Was it dear?"

"It was a great bargain, Aunt Mary."

"How much was it, son? Tell me, was it fifty?"

This Sunday I've returned to Aunt Mary from visiting Little Italy, where Deirdre's girls once strolled with their Italian father. I was there to read from the pages of this book to a pride of Soho artists—my fellow New Yorkers, but as foreign to me as Protestants are to Mary. I emerged from the subway into bakery-fresh air and pressed a buzzer at the steel door of the warehouse-turned-studio, and there, surrounded by an exhibition of paintings, I read two chapters to a gathering of posh pilgrims from the mid-West. They have transmogrified into New Yorkers, as the McCann girls did, but this isn't the New York of subways and cold-water flats. It's art and pastry and power lunches, studios and guerrilla uniforms, black coats, torn jeans, and navvy boots. And most of all, it's youth.

In tweed and tie, I rocked back and forth on the concrete floor, lifted my voice, and began, "Who would have thought, in 1960, when my brother's birth cramped our row house, expelling Aunt Mary back to Brooklyn. . . ."

Afterwards, the release of tension, the feel of something done, tainted with the embarrassment of having exposed so much in front of strangers. The audience mingled, clotting in small groups around the crepe-covered tables, but I stayed apart, shuffling from painting to painting, gawking, shelving the plastic wine cup and ferreting in my pocket for a flask. Among the splashes and rhomboids framed on the studio wall, I found and purchased the painting I have been writing toward.

If these electrified words have been exhumed from the ghost field and pressed and reproduced as the body of a printed page, then this painting, reproduced, has become a door between the living and the dead. The original hangs over my desk in my new house in Ohio, near a window that looks out at an absence where my imagination sets a gnarled frozen limb in early spring. And although, in the future I am writing toward, a reader fingers the image of paint and limb, I will tell now what I see.

Not Knowing, Relying on Intuition. I whisper the blue title while Mary gazes at the TV where bicycles and joggers traverse Michael Jordan's scalp. The words are cobalt, scorched by a flaming sky. Flame licks the sea, loamed with fish. The sea and sky—failed lovers, cloven brain, rhyme and madness, myth and particle, divided by a tree, not painted—a wood branch glued to canvas. The real, the painted. The living, the dead. Emerging from sea: a house, a casket built of sticks, half in painted sea, piercing the sky. Inside the house: a skeleton, electrified. Its heart flames like an icon; the skull is gaunt as a key.

I do not want to drown or burn. I want to wed the fish-loamed sea to burning sky. I want to close my eyes, open my mouth like a circus fire-eater and swallow the sky's heart. I want to speak on equal terms with the living and the dead. For this, I rely on a twig house glued to paint. I rely on a book whose cover reveals in miniature a casketed skeleton, flaming heart, and bone hands holding a tiny book—a book I rely on intuition to read.

The glued twig casket calls. I dive in, bringing with me Francis and Sarah McCann, Betty, Kay, Pet, even Deirdre—finally transplanted. All but Mary, who still faces the TV cathode sky. Behind me come all the artists fleeing to New York from the mid-West, and behind them, their stories intuited in paint. Last of all, Oisin himself dives in, his story one to sink us all.

Firstborn son of the colossal king of Ireland Finn MacCumhal, Oisin fell in love, and of course she was a Goddess, daughter of the faery host. "Look, son," said Finn, placing a huge paw on Oisin's shoulder, "I want you to be happy. You know that." He sneezed, uprooting a grove of trees. "Sorry, now. Son, stay with your own. You can't go gallivanting with that lot from the Sidhe. Take my word, it's no good."

But Oisin defied his father, eloped to Tir na nÓg, land of eternal youth, and there he sported for three nights in his lover's sea-borne bed. But in the land of youth he grew restless. Nothing but pure love, faeries, poetry. Absences called him: his father, friends, frozen tree limb, sky. Everything would be different now, he thought, now that he'd seen eternity. He had to return, at least for a little while.

And Niamh, Oisin's lover, hearing this, how she must have rolled her eyes. Men, she thought. Never satisfied, even in the land of youth. "You couldn't wait to be gone," she reminded him. "Now you have to run home and see your Da." He shrugged, shuffled his feet. So she shook her ringleted head and lent Oisin a horse to make the journey. Just one condition: don't set foot on land.

Perfect. A horse. Yes it had wings, could glide over the ocean. Oisin could mount this creature concocted of bird and myth and view from a great height the world he was born into, but the moment he touched ground—as he must touch, plot-driven—he shriveled, turning old. For he'd been gone not three nights as he believed, but three hundred years. That's what they do, these Goddesses: slow time.

Still, he didn't have to take a horse. He might have made it back another way, by making a tiny boat, a casket of twigs. He could have stretched out and gazed at the painted sky; listened to the sea lap at his ears, until color and rhythm and rhyme transfigured longing. Or maybe he should have heeded his father in the first place and stayed home. Many do. And those who refuse the journey have questions.

"So," says the tall beauty in strapless red after my New York reading, "What is it exactly you're doing? I mean, it's very poetic and all, but I don't get it. Who's your audience? Are you really Irish?"

And Finbar, on e-mail, "I know libel laws are looser in the States, but in Ireland, you'll be crucified."

And Brian, phoning after I sent him the manuscript, "Well, you've changed a few names, at least. That's something. I guess that makes this fiction. Huh? Well you better find out, Geraldo."

And Mary, who paddles in the land of youth, "Son, will we visit Flip soon?"

The world is flaming sky. Words are a dark sea, fish-loamed. And at the nexus—a boat, a casket, a tale. Aunt Mary sits in the living room, raising her arms from unplumbed depths. Alice Crimmins weeps in my father's arms. Genevieve cradles a ghost. Pet picks up the phone to make a call. The tale's not merely breath; the casket and the boat aren't just wood. They're spun of absences which flow forward as they ebb.

It's dusk now. Time to take Mary back, as far as we can go together. She mutters her doggerel as I wheel her out to the car, and I feel that tonight, in the crisp April air under the aching moon, we could drive far, to that place where threads unbraid—

Tir na nÓg, or Brooklyn, or a river whose waters rock back and forth like Flip rocking in front of a hi-fi.

Good-bye, son. Thanks for taking me out, I'm sorry to be such bother, good-bye, son. You'll be getting married now, I know you will. You'll marry soon, my Pet. I'll be alone. I had a grand fine house once too, you know. A gorgeous place. His mother paid. We sold it, ach, we sold it, me and Dick. His mother sent us the money to buy the house. In Hempstead, it was. Hempstead, on the Island. Far away on the Island, painted and all. We sold it, son, his mother, Protestant. When his mother came, he died. We sold the house. For fifty, we sold it, fifty thousand dollars. Did you pay fifty, son, fifty, for the house? He had a good job, as gardener, Dick did. As gardener on the Island, a good job. He sang. He loved to sing all the old songs. We called on him to sing and he always did. You wouldn't get a house like this in Brooklyn. Not a house like that, that big. Brian, maybe. Brian's the gorgeous one. He has a job. In Brooklyn he works, Brooklyn. But Flip's here. We drove, son, every Sunday after Mass, hours we used to drive, in the old Ford. We drove far out to the Island, Hempstead, Pet. Far off, and my poor dead husband Flip started to sing. My husband started singing the old songs. Nobody asked him even. He just started.

AFTERLIFE: POEMS

My business is circumference
—Emily Dickinson

WIRETAP

How could Detective Brady and his perky wife
storm upstairs to enforce lights out
when the blonde cross-legged on their sofa
had strangled her two children?
                              Perfectly safe,
I moled between the two top banister rails,
eavesdropped a spill, a laugh, and something clicking.
She must have sloshed her cocktail,
slipped her heels off. Soon,
muffled sobs, my father's tenor voice, *there there*.
Unthinkable now to slink back to my room,
dream murder mounting the pillowy stairs barefoot.
Maybe the girl puked up the night of June 23

or the boy sassed—maybe it was finally
too much—the late night waitressing, the boyfriends,
divorce in Queens in 1965.
Unthinkable—solitude a thing I couldn't bear—
still is—internal voices whisper *home*
and twice they've nearly had me married.
The cops had Alice Crimmins' Ford or something close
reliably witnessed cruising 3:30 AM.
Next day, they chalked one tiny corpse near Kew Gardens.
The other—the girl—nested in the weeds
of the World's Fair for two weeks.
Once a year, when my father picks me up at Kennedy,
we pass the silver skeleton Fair globe
without a word for that grim search,
the Crimmins trial—the sentence long since passed.
Although his Queens is a kind of wax museum
(at this gin mill Fuentes outbled Diaz,
at this ristorante Anthony Grace fell)
his famous case—the one they made a book—
this one he hates, because, he says,
my mother is not "perky" and some facts are fudged.
True, as the book says, mick bloodhounds
were bent on nailing that bitch Crimmins—
their eyes glazed over when she claimed
she checked the sleeping kids at 3 o'clock.
Instead, they teased clues from her beehive hairdo,
they sleuthed right through the shades
she donned for Daily News splash pics.
Kelly was stone stubborn, Pierig horny
to make second grade. They had the car,
they had the coroner pinning the first death
near 2 A.M. Still, they needed a mole—
someone they trusted, someone she would trust.

In *The Alice Crimmins Case*,
Detective Brady's manner is "confessional"—
and after twenty years, a heart attack,
cancer and four strokes, still is.
Clasping his hands, he hoods the dinner table
and the fact I am a liberal atheist
exudes from me like sweat
but never does the conversation stray
as far as who he is.
                            Mention the Crimmins case
and something inside him clicks,
something is welled in echoes,
something behind his eyes begins to spin
like the reel-to-reel that hunkered on his desk,
state-of-the-art, 1965. I grew up
too busy jerking off and freebasing
pure heresy at Fordham Prep
to eavesdrop cop tapes, but last month,
years after I stormed out the 53-28
screen door swearing new life, I spied,
wedged on a lost shelf in the basement
of a Berkeley used book shop, the familiar
discounted title. Sobs welled up
in that California cellar, most distant point
in the farthest orbit around Queens I'd dared,
so far I feared that if I took two steps,
nothing would pull back.
Yet, thumbing that pulp, I realized
my father had traveled farther.

What did it mean in 1965
to tape those sobs, then turn his back
on Kelly and Pierig, press *erase*?
Queens was a world honeycombed with generations,

a safe place for white men and most women.
What did it take to replay for the defense
proof the coroner fudged time of death?
The hack who wrote *The Alice Crimmins Case*
and juiced those sobs to hawk his schlock exposé
invents "two sleepless nights" for Detective Brady
before he wakes Alice's sad-sack lawyer.
But when I think of that ineffectual,
or just imaginary phone call
I see a door open and my father
take two steps into nothing—
but for all my traveling, I'll never know—
and though I want him not to go on
being him, me being me,
I haven't stopped, nor found a way
to tell all this to anyone I love.

FIRST BORN

THE day the four McCann girls were shown Brooklyn
and told that beneath their feet were rivers and tunnels,
another fleet of trams, a whole underground city—
that was the day they realized they'd need me.

They could translate pence to nickels,
knew *mince* meant *raisin*, but one look
at the brickwork, the smoking girders—one look
at their small blue parents inching under the neon
storming the sky, and all but the baby sensed
they'd need an American—rich, educated,
tall if possible. But where to find one in the grease-
japped kitchens, in the kiosks, in the velvet sacristies?

On Sundays, Paddies in sloped work caps
leered at McCann's front stoop, greasers
sharked the boulevards, and Jews, garbed as mad priests,
muttered and cawed along the lanes of Prospect Park.
But the only way to get an American was to make one.

Mary was eldest so she tried first, but she barely had time
to squint at the house I'd rent one day
with turrets and stained glass windows opening into pine
    limbs
before the gardener she married,
whose tenor voice still trills in McCann memory,
died of rare cancer and their girl-child
started to swipe coins and grow black
crooked teeth not like me at all.

Then Betty the prim one entered
the plush mouth of the Savoy movie house
and when she exited daylight
swelled to rubies in her bleary sight, and that night
in her pillow she saw Africa: Bogart's bone deep
American gaze, and she, shimmying in the dream
out of her wool skirt, patting her curls.
All that summer she peered back
into the scum-white Coney Island surf
and then this Elizabeth, who skipped
over sidewalk cracks and steam-ironed her underwear—
she fainted, flailing the flexed waves
until a navvy flung his shoes in after,
and they lived like that, fainting and belting each other
while forty years skimmed by like a flat stone
and now she's babbling this fractured tale to me,
the sea meanwhile having shrunk to a damp shell,
but she's sure—my aunt—and still furious

that it was me thrashed out of her womb like a knife
(I nod, purr *sure*) and when she stiffens, spits out
that I fecked off the wrong way to some war,
came back someone else, I steal a glance
at my cousin's military snapshot taped
to the steel nursing home bed frame and swear
when it comes to this between myself
and me we'll shoot each other.

Then it was Kay who coaxed a wraith by jitterbugging
her flame fingernails; together they raptured
bars and K. of C. Halls then boogied home to make a me
Christ would mistake for his transfigured twin;
but I'd been craved so many times it was born
smudged—their whelp—padding the threadbare rug
in orthopedic shoes, getting religion,
soiling his musical necktie in the kitty litter.

And that left Pet the youngest who dreamt at first
of turrets and Bogart but finally
it was the dark she loved, mirrored
when she closed her eyes and pulled
a man down into it. That was the traveling then,
she could glide anywhere, the rivers and tunnels
farther than she'd ever seen or thought—no fear,
no need—and when she looked up I was gone—
for all the scams they brooded—
I'd slipped, easy as a hanky through a ring,
though it must be
a sliver of me's lodged in the obscure god
who sprays graffiti and puffs black soot
on the crust of Brooklyn,
wildly fanning his worshippers back to life.

LAGOS

My younger brother, orphaned, phones
past midnight from the West to warn
that Lagos is fatal to travelers.

These months I haven't stopped moving
and even in sleep my eyes
need a constant downward
and eastward pull.
                        He read the warning sign
in three languages at L.A.X., and says
I must not go.
                I listen
but can't follow anything that gives up

short of the far margin.

                            When the doctors

finally gave up, my mother was elevated

to the top floor and I was let

sleep with her in an empty wing.

What dream makes me fear rising?

I need midnight to be spirited

over silences like sidewalk cracks

until sounds slip destination

and walking is just falling

in step.

             I could easily have gone

with my first brother: this my mother

murmurs in my dreams

in morphine tongue.

But I thought I was eldest.

                          These months,

booze and book gloss honeycomb

the inside of the skull.

                   Downward

and eastward, Lagos

is a hive of unknown millions guidebooks

compare unfavorably to Cocytus.

                         Sleeping

in the hospital with my mother

was closer than I've ever been

to anyone though I seldom touched her.

She didn't always know

which one I was—sometimes she thought

I wanted blood so she would turn

her head into the pillow and hold
out her left arm.
            I was a blue
baby, transfused eight times
in my first two weeks of life.
My mother called me
distant and often joked
I was a changeling.
              At night
in the empty wing I sang
her songs and sometimes words
channeled through me from the honeycomb
of rooms below my feet.
               God knows.
Is that good? I'll be right back.

My brother and I crashed into each other
from opposite shores each cigarette break.

It was me stranded in California then
and I phoned in almost every breath.

My voyage is conducted by the eyes,
but memory seeps, silting up
the delta of the optic nerve. Then
words give up.
            The doctors
gave up after the third intubation.
Intubation is a word but when remembered
it is my mother's face incarnate,
it means shut off from air and speech.

A priest translated—sometimes my mother
thought I was this priest

and turned toward me like a sunflower
toward light.
                         In Lagos
traffic and gas fumes murder sleep.
I have touched down
in a city of three languages,
all slurred.
                         If only to recall
my mother's face turning toward light
I'll translate now: trauma
means suffering if it's someone else's,
even if you once nestled in her wing.

In Lagos my eyes move downward
and eastward against dreams.
                         Movement
is a mantra.
                         Dopamine is a number
telling how tight the human network's
stretched.
                         If you've seen Lagos
traffic you know what it means
when tubes are forced down a living
throat.
                         Memory seizes.
                         Sleeping
with my mother means
her death.
              If
my father's low sperm count
hadn't kept me formless until after
World War II experiments with RH factors,
I'd have choked on my own blood.
                         Death

can be hilarious.
> The last thing
she said was, *Don't cry you're getting me
all wet.* And before that—
she whispers it each night into
my sleep—*Where is
my firstborn?*
> She liked morphine
and when she wasn't being made
to breath by machine, she said
reproachfully, *This
is what drugs should be for.*
> Can secrets
conjoin us without flesh?

The doctors said don't worry
how horrible it looks, she won't
remember.
> When I
remember, the earth skids
and veers, the mind
seizes and I'm jumbled back
in intense sun under the Ujiji
mango tree where Dr. Livingstone
encountered Henry Morton Stanley.
> Coincidence
sparks a fleeting sexual joy.
> I travel
ear to the vanishing,
the way my brother
records his kids shilling ditties
on his answering machine.
> Sometimes
in rage we call each other

Father in a kind of mythopoetic
Who's On First.
     I didn't sleep with my mother
but lay awake listening to her breath
like fast spondees; and each breath
depended on the fiction
of one thing following another.
       From Lagos,
I follow the river to the Emir's Palace
near the ford where Mungo Park drowned.
          Can tides

quell fear?
   I returned
to the top floor and the doctor
was already there—in hospitals
they're kings—it's unbelievable
they can walk under the weight
of so much awe.

He was diffident; he'd risen
to Marin General from the Bronx
and he saw this Brooklyn mother and her son
and felt, maybe, just faintly,
that but for luck he might have been born
me.
  Me, that is, the one,
       by miracle,
blue-blooded, christened
maybe in past lives as
Mungo or Henry Morton—
       that's the trick—to step
into that one
of a billion incarnations that won't
madden.

       The doctor said
he admired poetry
             and for that
incarnated instant I felt human
as if my mother's body were still
free, her gaze
deepening as the jacarandas brightened
in the window—
             there's nothing like Marin—
the hospital cafeteria is a bistro—

and I would have done anything,
anything in the world to please
him, to coax his words
into my mother's living face.
             The Emir's
Palace has no running water, but his word
knits ninety villages together.
             Dreams
ascend to congest the pineal gland.
             Lagos
is a labyrinth—it swallowed
eleven billion dollars in windfall profits
from the Gulf War and it's still
famished.
         Even the desert's
breath, the harmattan,
dies in its maw.
         I returned
to the top floor from a quick smoke
and the elevator hissed open as usual.

Choosing that my mother die
instead of breathe

by machine is a memory, but dreams spasm
silent as heat lightning—I can wind up
anywhere unless my eyes
keep moving.
        I travel to describe
an arc: an ark rocked by cloud-
exploding storm.
        My father died
three weeks before my mother
visited California, and on days
the morphine thinned and she remembered
that he went without a word or a glance back,
she said she felt like a stranded Baucis.
                  One night
the capital was spirited from Lagos
to the beautiful planned city of Abuja.

I found my mother naked
in intensive care, her face
wedged between gurney
and night table, her right arm spasming
like a crippled moth.

It was the first time
I ever lay down with her.
It was the first time nothing mattered,
just *live*.
      Heat rises
from Lagos dirt streets past midnight.
Even at night my skin itches and burns.

In the hospital my mother talked with ghosts
using her right hand as a phone.
I learned by eavesdropping

on morphine I am not
her first.
　　　　Livingstone missed
the true source of the Nile, but followers
carried his bier reverently to the sea.

Let the sea churn.

When the Emir entered, his peacock
miraculously unfurled, each quill
distinct, the great fan sweeping
the Aegean eyes in a design of moons.

My mother always wanted to be a wren.
She sang herself a cautionary lullaby
about a mother who murdered her baby
and was hanged.
　　　　　I sing to remember
one thing following another, but I can't
thread words.
　　　　　My mother never abandoned
her first ghost.
　　　　He lived
with the wrong blood only
a week, and so I took
his name.
　　　Lying
with her in intensive care and later
with her body breathing
from memory on the top
floor, I only
wanted to unsleeve my skin.

The string they call

the lifeline is frayed blue.
Maybe I'll unfurl.
       No one
knows exactly what happened.

My mother thought she was going to see
her mother, she said her mother
loved her the way she loved me, but by then
I wasn't sure exactly who she talked to.
Seven villages claim the spot
where Mungo Park died.
       When my elder
brother died, he left
a trace of longing deepening
in my eyes.
       I found him
forty years too late as in
some treacly Dickens plotline
winged with harps.
       From Lagos,
America seems heaven. For funerals,
they slaughter seven cows, but their
cows look like starved kine of Exodus.

Undertakers have an underground
air network—they drain
the blood, apotheosize clients
20,000 feet, then sink six—like
counter-clockwise Christs.
       Maybe I'll go.
Maybe a brother needs me. I don't know
where I'd be with my own blood.

There are days I prefer the swimming pools,

the palms, the sweet order of Abuja.

One morning I rose to the empty wing
and she was gone
and though she'd wandered
the morphine labyrinth
for weeks, I don't know
what broke free, if anything
ascended westward, or if
she looked back, but if
this was
my sweet Euridice,
there was nobody there to wave goodbye to.

ABOUT THE AUTHOR

Philip Brady was born and raised in New York City and educated at Bucknell University, the University of Delaware, San Francisco State University, and SUNY Binghamton. Author of two books of poems, his work has appeared in many journals in America and Ireland and has been translated into Polish, Spanish, and Hebrew. He has won four Ohio Arts Council Individual Artists Fellowships, a Thayer Fellowship from New York State, the Snyder Prize from Ashland Poetry Press, and residencies at Yaddo, the Headlands Center for the Arts, Fundacion Valparaiso, Hawthornden Castle, the Soros Center for the Arts, the Ragdale Foundation, the Millay Colony, the Hambidge Center, and the Virginia Center for the Creative Arts. Brady has taught at University College Cork, Ireland, and, as a Peace Corps Volunteer, at the University of Lubumbashi. Currently, he is a professor of English and Creative Writing at Youngstown State University, where he directs the Poetry Center.

ASHLAND POETRY PRESS